LEARNING DART FOR FLUTTER DEVELOPMENT

Create Mobile Apps Fast

THOMPSON CARTER

TABLE OF CONTENTS

Introduction

Learning Dart for Flutter Development: Create Mobile Apps Fast"

In today's world, mobile apps are an essential part of nearly every business, entertainment, and social interaction. With millions of apps available across app stores, building an efficient, cross-platform mobile application is more important than ever. As a result, choosing the right tools and frameworks is key to ensuring success in the mobile development space.

This book, **"Learning Dart for Flutter Development: Create Mobile Apps Fast"**, is designed for developers who want to create powerful, high-performance mobile applications using **Flutter** and the **Dart programming language**. Whether you're an experienced developer new to Flutter or a beginner aiming to learn mobile app development, this book provides a step-by-step guide to building real-world apps with ease.

Flutter has rapidly become one of the most popular frameworks for building natively compiled applications for mobile, web, and desktop from a single codebase. Its rich set of pre-built widgets, fast development cycle, and strong community support make it an ideal choice for developers aiming to deliver beautiful, responsive, and high-performance applications. But behind Flutter's easy-to-use UI lies **Dart**, the programming language powering it. Learning Dart is crucial for unlocking the full potential of Flutter and writing efficient, maintainable code that scales with your app.

Why Learn Dart and Flutter?

Flutter stands out from other mobile development frameworks due to its **performance** and **cross-platform capabilities**. Instead of writing separate codebases for iOS and Android, Flutter allows you to write a single codebase that works across multiple platforms. However, to take full advantage of Flutter, you need to master Dart, which provides the foundation for Flutter's reactive programming model.

Dart is a modern, fast, object-oriented language that supports features such as just-in-time (JIT) and ahead-of-time (AOT) compilation. It's designed to be easy to learn, especially for developers familiar with JavaScript, Java, or C#. Dart's clean syntax and strong typing system make it an excellent choice for building scalable and high-performance apps.

Flutter's ability to deliver **native performance** with a **single codebase** has made it the go-to solution for many startups, enterprises, and individual developers. Additionally, Flutter's built-in Material Design and Cupertino widgets make it easy to create beautiful UIs that adhere to platform-specific design principles.

What This Book Offers

This book goes beyond simply introducing you to the fundamentals of Dart and Flutter. It's designed to help you create mobile apps **fast**—from start to finish—by providing you with practical examples, in-depth explanations, and real-world applications.

By the time you finish this book, you will be able to:

- Understand the Dart programming language and use it effectively for Flutter development.
- Build responsive UIs using Flutter's rich set of widgets and layout mechanisms.
- Integrate external APIs, manage app data, and handle persistent storage with modern tools.
- Implement state management techniques to keep your app's data consistent across screens.
- Optimize your app's performance, debug issues, and test your app effectively.
- Deploy your Flutter app to the Google Play Store and Apple App Store for a global audience.

Real-world examples are provided throughout the book to demonstrate how the concepts covered can be used in practical scenarios. Whether you're building a simple to-do list app, a product catalog, or a fully functional e-commerce app, this book provides the tools and knowledge needed to bring your app ideas to life.

Who Should Read This Book?

This book is aimed at:

- **Beginner developers**: If you're new to programming or mobile development, this book will walk you through all the basics of Dart and Flutter in a clear, approachable manner.

- **Intermediate developers**: If you have experience with other languages or frameworks (such as JavaScript, React Native, Swift, or Kotlin), this book will teach you how to transition into Flutter, and help you leverage the unique features of Dart.

- **Experienced mobile developers**: If you're already familiar with mobile app development but want to master Flutter and Dart, this book offers advanced topics and best practices to help you level up your skills.

What You Will Learn

Throughout the chapters, you'll learn essential concepts such as:

1. **Dart Programming Fundamentals**: The building blocks of Dart, including variables, data types, control flow, functions, and object-oriented programming concepts like classes and inheritance.

2. **Flutter Basics**: Setting up a Flutter environment, understanding widgets, and building user interfaces.

3. **State Management**: Techniques like setState, Provider, and Riverpod to handle dynamic data.

4. **Working with APIs**: Making network requests, handling asynchronous data, and integrating third-party APIs.

5. **Database Management**: Using SQLite for local data storage and Firebase for cloud solutions.

6. **Animations**: Adding smooth, interactive animations and transitions to your Flutter app.

7. **Advanced Topics**: Including performance optimization, architecture patterns, security, and app deployment to Google Play and the App Store.

By the end of this book, you will have built several fully functioning mobile applications using Flutter and Dart, equipped with the skills necessary to tackle any project, whether it's for personal use or as a professional developer.

Why Flutter and Dart?

- **Cross-platform development**: Write your app once and deploy it across Android, iOS, and even web or desktop platforms.

- **Performance**: Native-like performance thanks to Flutter's direct compilation to ARM or x86 code, and Dart's AOT compilation.

- **Rich set of Widgets**: Flutter provides an extensive collection of pre-built widgets that make it easy to create beautiful, responsive UIs.

- **Fast Development**: With features like Hot Reload, you can instantly see changes in your app without losing its state, making the development process faster and more iterative.

Final Thoughts

Whether you're an aspiring mobile app developer or an experienced programmer looking to expand your skill set, **"Learning Dart for Flutter Development: Create Mobile Apps Fast"** is your comprehensive guide to mastering Flutter and Dart. Packed with clear explanations, practical examples, and real-world applications, this book will empower you to build high-quality, production-ready mobile apps in no time.

Get ready to embark on your journey of Flutter development and unlock the power of building beautiful, fast, and scalable apps for both Android and iOS, using the cutting-edge tools that Flutter and Dart offer.

Chapter 1: Introduction to Mobile App Development

What is Mobile App Development?

Mobile app development refers to the process of designing, building, testing, and deploying software applications for mobile devices, including smartphones and tablets. Mobile apps can range from simple utility apps, such as calculators or weather apps, to complex platforms like social media, games, or enterprise applications.

Mobile apps are typically built using one of three approaches:

- **Native apps**: These are platform-specific apps developed for a particular operating system (iOS or Android). They're written in languages like Swift (iOS) or Kotlin/Java (Android), and they leverage the full capabilities of the mobile device.

- **Web apps**: These are essentially websites optimized for mobile devices. They run within a browser, are written in web technologies (HTML, CSS, JavaScript), and do not require installation from an app store.
- **Cross-platform apps**: These apps can run on both iOS and Android from a single codebase. They are typically built with frameworks like Flutter, React Native, and Xamarin, and they offer a balance of performance and code efficiency.

In this book, we'll focus on **Flutter**, a popular framework for building cross-platform mobile apps.

Why Dart and Flutter Are Ideal for Mobile Apps

Flutter is an open-source UI framework created by Google, which uses the Dart programming language to build natively compiled applications for mobile, web, and desktop from a single codebase. It has gained massive popularity due to its ability to deliver high-quality, performant apps with a unified codebase.

Dart is the programming language behind Flutter. While Dart itself isn't as widely known as some other languages, it has been specifically designed for building fast, reactive apps. Let's break down why **Dart and Flutter** are ideal for mobile app development:

- **Single Codebase, Multiple Platforms**: Flutter allows developers to write a single codebase and deploy apps across multiple platforms like iOS, Android, and even web and desktop. This drastically reduces development time and cost.

- **Fast Development with Hot Reload**: One of the standout features of Flutter is "Hot Reload," which allows developers to instantly see the effects of code changes without restarting the app. This speeds up the development cycle and makes it easier to experiment with UI changes.

- **Native Performance**: Flutter apps are compiled to native ARM code, which means they can run with high performance on mobile devices, even with complex animations or graphics.

- **Beautiful UIs with Customization**: Flutter comes with a rich set of pre-built widgets that help create a visually appealing, responsive UI. If the pre-built widgets don't meet your needs, you can easily customize them or even build your own from scratch.

- **Growing Ecosystem**: Flutter has a large and growing community of developers, libraries, and tools. The ecosystem continues to improve with every release, and Google's backing ensures the framework will evolve with the latest mobile development trends.

- **Rich Documentation and Learning Resources**: As a developer, you'll have access to comprehensive documentation, tutorials, and an active community that can help you solve problems and improve your app.

Key Benefits of Using Flutter

1. **Cross-Platform Development**:
   - **Save Time and Resources**: Instead of writing separate code for iOS and Android, you only need one codebase. Flutter allows you to deploy to multiple platforms like iOS, Android, and web with minimal changes.
   - **Consistency Across Devices**: Flutter ensures that your app will look the same and work consistently on both iOS and Android devices, preventing the fragmentation issues often seen with native development.

2. **Faster Time to Market**:
   - **Hot Reload**: Developers can instantly see changes in the app, which makes experimenting with different UI designs and functionality much faster. This allows teams to iterate quickly and deliver a finished product in less time.

o **Single Codebase Maintenance**: Managing a single codebase for multiple platforms is easier than maintaining separate codebases for iOS and Android.

3. **High-Quality Native Performance**:

   o Flutter's apps are compiled directly to native ARM code for performance that's comparable to native apps, ensuring a smooth and responsive user experience.

   o Flutter integrates easily with platform-specific code when you need access to native APIs, further enhancing performance.

4. **Customizable, Beautiful UIs**:

   o Flutter allows you to design highly custom, attractive, and adaptive UIs. You can use pre-built widgets or create your own, and the framework gives you full control over the app's layout and animations.

   o The rich set of material and Cupertino widgets ensures that your app follows the design principles of both Android and iOS.

5. **Strong Community and Google Support**:

   o Google's support for Flutter ensures continuous updates and improvements to the framework. The strong community behind Flutter contributes to an ever-growing number of libraries and resources.

- Whether you need to find tutorials, solutions for issues, or third-party packages to extend Flutter's functionality, the community will help you find what you need.

6. **Integration with Firebase**:

- Flutter works seamlessly with Firebase, Google's Backend-as-a-Service (BaaS) platform, providing easy-to-implement solutions for authentication, real-time databases, analytics, and more.

7. **Future-Proof and Flexible**:

- With Google's backing, Flutter has a long-term future. Additionally, because Flutter is based on Dart, it's well-suited for future trends like Internet of Things (IoT) and other emerging platforms.

In the following chapters, we'll dive deeper into Dart's syntax and features, and how it integrates with Flutter to bring your mobile app ideas to life. But first, let's understand how to set up Dart and Flutter in your development environment and create your first app.

Chapter 2: Getting Started with Dart Programming Language

Introduction to Dart

Dart is an open-source, general-purpose programming language developed by Google. It is primarily used for building mobile, desktop, and web applications, with a strong emphasis on performance and ease of use. Dart's syntax is easy to learn, especially for developers familiar with other object-oriented programming languages like JavaScript, Java, or C#.

Key Features of Dart:

- **Object-Oriented**: Dart is purely object-oriented, which means everything in Dart is an object (even numbers, strings, and functions).
- **Strong Typing**: Dart is statically typed, meaning variables have a defined type, but it also supports type inference, so you don't always have to declare the type explicitly.
- **Asynchronous Programming**: Dart provides robust support for asynchronous programming using async and await, which is critical for smooth app performance, particularly in mobile development.

Dart serves as the foundation for Flutter, which makes it essential to have a solid grasp of the language before diving into Flutter development.

Setting Up Your Development Environment

To start developing with Dart, you need to set up your development environment. This involves installing Dart SDK, choosing an Integrated Development Environment (IDE), and configuring everything for smooth development. Here's a step-by-step guide:

1. Install Dart SDK:

- Go to the official Dart website: https://dart.dev/get-dart
- Follow the installation instructions for your operating system (Windows, macOS, Linux).
- After installation, verify that Dart is properly installed by running the command dart --version in your terminal or command prompt.

2. IDE Setup: While you can use any text editor for Dart development, it's highly recommended to use an IDE that supports Dart and Flutter to streamline the development process. Some popular IDEs are:

- **Visual Studio Code**: A lightweight, fast editor with Dart and Flutter plugins available.
- **Android Studio**: A more heavyweight IDE but ideal if you plan to also develop Android apps.
- **IntelliJ IDEA**: Another powerful option for Dart and Flutter development.

After choosing your IDE, make sure to install the necessary Dart and Flutter plugins/extensions. These provide syntax highlighting, code completion, debugging support, and other features to improve your development workflow.

3. Verify Installation: To ensure everything is set up correctly, run the following commands in your terminal or command prompt:

- dart --version to check Dart's version.
- flutter doctor to check if Flutter is installed correctly and to verify the health of your environment.

First Dart Program: A Simple Console App

Now that your development environment is set up, let's write a simple Dart program to ensure everything works as expected.

1. **Create a New Dart File:**
   - Open your IDE or text editor, create a new file, and name it main.dart.

2. **Write Your First Dart Program:** Copy and paste the following code into your main.dart file:

dart

```dart
void main() {
  print('Hello, Dart!');
}
```

Explanation:

- void main(): This is the entry point of every Dart application. It's similar to the main() function in other languages like C and Java.
- print(): This is a Dart function that outputs the string Hello, Dart! to the console.

3. **Run the Program:** Open your terminal or IDE and run the program using the following command:

bash

```bash
dart run main.dart
```

You should see Hello, Dart! printed in the console.

This simple example demonstrates the basics of Dart syntax and how to run a Dart program. Understanding these fundamentals will give you the foundation to explore more complex topics as you begin your journey into Flutter development.

This chapter lays the groundwork for Dart programming, so in the next chapter, we will dive deeper into Dart's core concepts like variables, functions, and data types.

Chapter 3: Introduction to Flutter

What is Flutter and How Does It Work?

Flutter is a popular open-source UI framework developed by Google for building natively compiled applications for mobile, web, and desktop from a single codebase. It enables developers to create beautiful and high-performance applications with a consistent look and feel across platforms, including iOS and Android.

Key Concepts Behind Flutter:

- **Widgets**: The core building blocks of Flutter applications are widgets. Everything in a Flutter app is a widget—from the structure of the app to the layout, buttons, and text. Widgets can be stateful (holding mutable state) or stateless (fixed, unchanging).

- **Single Codebase**: One of Flutter's standout features is that developers can write code once and deploy it across multiple platforms (iOS, Android, Web, Desktop) without needing to rewrite it for each one. Flutter achieves this by compiling to native ARM code for mobile platforms, which results in excellent performance.

- **Dart Language**: Flutter is built with Dart, a fast, modern programming language that is easy to learn and highly productive for mobile app development. Dart provides tools and libraries that help developers create seamless, high-performance UIs.

How Does Flutter Work?

- **Widget Rendering**: Flutter doesn't use the native platform's UI elements. Instead, it provides its own high-performance rendering engine (Skia) to draw widgets directly onto the screen. This enables consistent performance across devices.
- **Hot Reload**: Flutter's hot reload feature allows developers to see changes instantly without restarting the app. This speeds up development and testing significantly, making it ideal for rapid iteration.
- **Skia Rendering Engine**: Flutter's Skia engine is highly optimized for mobile devices, ensuring smooth animations, complex graphics, and fast performance even on lower-end devices.

Setting Up Flutter and Running Your First Flutter App

To get started with Flutter, you'll need to install the Flutter SDK and set up your development environment. Below are the steps:

1. **Install Flutter SDK**:
   - Download the Flutter SDK from the official website (https://flutter.dev).

- o Follow the installation instructions based on your operating system (Windows, macOS, or Linux).

2. **Install an IDE**: Flutter supports two main IDEs:

   - o **Android Studio**: This is the official IDE for Flutter development. It provides full support for Flutter, including debugging, code completion, and a simulator.
   - o **VS Code**: A lightweight alternative to Android Studio, with Flutter plugins available for fast development.

3. **Install Android Studio/VS Code and Flutter Plugin**:

   - o If using Android Studio, install the Flutter and Dart plugins to get full support for Flutter development.
   - o For VS Code, install the Flutter extension from the marketplace.

4. **Set up an Emulator or Physical Device**:

   - o For iOS, you'll need Xcode and an iOS simulator.
   - o For Android, install Android Emulator or connect a physical Android device for testing.

5. **Create a Flutter Project**:

   - o Open your IDE and use the command flutter create your_project_name to create a new Flutter project.
   - o Navigate to the project folder and run flutter run in the terminal to see the default Flutter template app in action.

Anatomy of a Flutter App

Understanding the structure of a Flutter application is essential for developing your own apps. Below is a breakdown of the main components in a typical Flutter app:

1. **Main Function (main.dart):** Every Flutter application starts with the main() function. This is where your app's entry point resides. Inside the main() function, you usually call runApp(), which is responsible for inflating the widget tree.

   dart

   ```dart
   void main() {
     runApp(MyApp());
   }
   ```

2. **The Root Widget:** In most apps, the root widget is usually a StatelessWidget or a StatefulWidget. It defines the top-level structure of the app, such as the navigation, themes, and initial screen.

   Example:

   dart

   ```dart
   class MyApp extends StatelessWidget {
     @override
     Widget build(BuildContext context) {
   ```

```
  return MaterialApp(
    title: 'Flutter Demo',
    theme: ThemeData(primarySwatch: Colors.blue),
    home: MyHomePage(),
  );
 }
}
```

3. **The Widget Tree**:
Flutter apps are built using a widget tree. Every widget in Flutter is part of this tree, which determines how the UI should be displayed. The root widget typically points to other widgets, like the home screen, which in turn points to widgets like buttons, text fields, etc.

Example of the Widget Tree:

dart

```
class MyHomePage extends StatelessWidget {
 @override
 Widget build(BuildContext context) {
  return Scaffold(
   appBar: AppBar(
    title: Text("Flutter Demo"),
   ),
   body: Center(
    child: Text("Hello, Flutter!"),
   ),
  );
```

```
}
}
```

4. **Stateless vs Stateful Widgets**:

   ○ **StatelessWidget**: This is used for widgets that don't depend on mutable state. Once they are built, their UI doesn't change.

   ○ **StatefulWidget**: This is used when the widget's state can change over time, like interacting with the user or fetching data.

Example of a StatefulWidget:

dart

```
class CounterApp extends StatefulWidget {
 @override
 _CounterAppState createState() => _CounterAppState();
}

class _CounterAppState extends State<CounterApp> {
 int _counter = 0;

 void _incrementCounter() {
  setState(() {
   _counter++;
  });
 }

 @override
```

```
Widget build(BuildContext context) {
  return Scaffold(
    appBar: AppBar(title: Text('Counter App')),
    body: Center(
      child: Column(
        mainAxisAlignment: MainAxisAlignment.center,
        children: <Widget>[
          Text('Button pressed $_counter times'),
          ElevatedButton(
            onPressed: _incrementCounter,
            child: Text('Increment'),
          ),
        ],
      ),
    ),
  );
}
}
```

5. **Layouts and Widgets**:

   o **Container**: A simple widget used to create boxes for other widgets.

   o **Row** and **Column**: Layout widgets used to arrange children horizontally (Row) or vertically (Column).

   o **Scaffold**: A layout widget that implements the basic material design visual layout structure, including app bars, drawers, floating action buttons, etc.

6. **The   Build   Method**:

The build() method is crucial in Flutter. It describes how to render the widget tree in terms of UI components. It's invoked whenever the state changes or the widget is first created.

Example:

dart

```
@override
Widget build(BuildContext context) {
  return Scaffold(
    appBar: AppBar(title: Text('Flutter App')),
    body: Center(child: Text('Welcome to Flutter!')),
  );
}
```

This chapter has introduced you to the basics of Flutter—what it is, how it works, and how to set it up on your system. You've also learned about the fundamental structure of a Flutter app, including its main components and how to start building your own apps.

Chapter 4: Dart Fundamentals: Variables, Data Types, and Operators

---

Variables and Constants in Dart

In Dart, variables are used to store data that can be modified or retrieved later. You can declare variables using the var, final, or const keywords depending on the intended use of the variable. Let's break down the differences:

- **var**: The most flexible way to declare a variable. Dart uses type inference to determine the type of the variable at runtime based on the assigned value. Once the type is set, it cannot be changed.

  dart

  ```
  var name = 'John'; // Dart infers that 'name' is of type String
  name = 'Alice';    // This works because it's still a String
  ```

- **final**: Declares a variable whose value cannot be changed once it's assigned, but the value is determined at runtime.

  dart

  ```
  final pi = 3.14; // 'pi' is a constant value that cannot be reassigned
  ```

- **const**: Declares a compile-time constant, meaning the value must be known at compile time and cannot be changed during execution.

dart

const maxItems = 100; // 'maxItems' is a compile-time constant

Working with Data Types

Dart is a statically typed language, meaning you must specify the type of data your variables hold, but Dart can also infer the type if not explicitly declared. Dart supports both **primitive** and **user-defined** data types.

Common Data Types in Dart:

- **Numbers**: Dart supports both integers (int) and floating-point numbers (double).

dart

```
int age = 25;
double price = 99.99;
```

- **String**: A sequence of characters. Strings are immutable, meaning once created, they cannot be changed.

dart

```dart
String name = 'John';
```

- **Booleans**: Represent true or false values.

dart

```dart
bool isFlutterAwesome = true;
```

- **Lists (Arrays)**: An ordered collection of items.

dart

```dart
List<String> fruits = ['Apple', 'Banana', 'Cherry'];
```

- **Maps (Dictionaries/Objects)**: A collection of key-value pairs.

dart

```dart
Map<String, int> ageMap = {'John': 25, 'Alice': 30};
```

- **Runes**: For working with Unicode characters.

dart

```dart
var heart = '\u2665';  // Unicode representation of heart symbol
```

Dart also supports **nullable types**, allowing you to specify that a variable can either hold a value of a certain type or null (useful for optional values or missing data).

dart

String? nullableString = null; // Nullable string

Operators in Dart

Operators in Dart perform various operations on variables and values. Dart supports a wide range of operators, similar to those in other programming languages.

Arithmetic Operators:

- +, -, *, /, % (addition, subtraction, multiplication, division, modulus)

dart

```
int sum = 10 + 5;  // 15
double quotient = 20.0 / 4.0;  // 5.0
```

Relational Operators:

- ==, !=, >, <, >=, <= (equality, inequality, greater than, less than, greater than or equal to, less than or equal to)

dart

```
bool isEqual = (5 == 5);  // true
bool isGreaterThan = (10 > 5);  // true
```

Logical Operators:

- &&, ||, ! (AND, OR, NOT)

dart

```dart
bool isAdult = true;
bool isStudent = false;
bool canEnter = isAdult && !isStudent;  // true
```

Assignment Operators:

- =, +=, -=, *=, /=, %=

dart

```dart
int counter = 10;
counter += 5;  // counter is now 15
```

Cascade Notation (..):

A powerful feature in Dart that allows you to call multiple methods on the same object, one after another, without repeating the object reference.

dart

```dart
var buffer = StringBuffer();
buffer..write('Hello')..write(' World');
print(buffer.toString());  // Outputs 'Hello World'
```

Conditional Operator (?:):

The conditional (ternary) operator allows for concise conditional expressions.

dart

```dart
int age = 20;
```

String message = (age >= 18) ? 'Adult' : 'Minor';

print(message); // Outputs 'Adult'

Null-aware Operators:

- ?.: Calls a method or accesses a property on an object only if it is not null.

- ??: Returns the right-hand operand if the left-hand operand is null.

- ??=: Assigns a value to a variable only if that variable is currently null.

Example:

dart

```
String? name;
print(name?.length);  // null (no error if 'name' is null)
name ??= 'Guest';     // Assign 'Guest' to 'name' only if it's null
```

In this chapter, we covered the basics of Dart programming, starting with how to declare variables and constants. You learned about Dart's key data types like numbers, strings, booleans, lists, and maps. Additionally, we explored operators such as arithmetic, relational, logical, and assignment operators, along with advanced features like cascade notation and null-aware operators. These fundamentals will serve as the building blocks for more complex Flutter app development in the following chapters.

Let's continue to explore how Dart interacts with Flutter to create beautiful and functional mobile applications.

Chapter 5: Control Flow: If-Else, Loops, and Switch Statements

Conditional Statements: if, else, switch

Control flow statements help direct the flow of execution in a program based on conditions. In Dart, the primary control flow statements are if, else, and switch.

1. **if and else Statements:**

    The if statement is used to execute code only if a certain condition is true. The else statement provides an alternative execution path when the condition is false.

    dart

    ```dart
    int age = 20;
    if (age >= 18) {
      print("You are an adult.");
    } else {
      print("You are a minor.");
    }
    ```

    o   The above code checks if age is 18 or more and prints whether the person is an adult or a minor.

2. **switch Statement:**

The switch statement evaluates a variable and executes the corresponding block of code based on the value of the variable. It's more efficient than using multiple if-else conditions when there are several potential values to check.

dart

```
String day = 'Monday';
switch (day) {
  case 'Monday':
    print('Start of the work week!');
    break;
  case 'Saturday':
  case 'Sunday':
    print('Weekend!');
    break;
  default:
    print('Midweek day');
}
```

o The above example evaluates the value of the day variable and prints a message based on its value. The break statement is crucial to exit the switch block after executing the matching case.

Loops: *for, while, do-while*

Loops allow repetitive execution of code based on certain conditions. Dart offers three main types of loops:

1. **for Loop:**

   A for loop is used when you know beforehand how many times you want to iterate through a block of code.

   dart

   ```
   for (int i = 0; i < 5; i++) {
     print('Iteration $i');
   }
   ```

   - This loop starts with i = 0 and runs until i < 5. The value of i increments with each iteration.

2. **while Loop:**

   A while loop runs as long as the specified condition is true. If the condition is initially false, the loop doesn't execute.

   dart

   ```
   int count = 0;
   while (count < 5) {
     print('Count: $count');
     count++;
   }
   ```

o   This loop will continue to run as long as count is less than 5.

3. **do-while Loop:**

Similar to the while loop, except that the condition is evaluated **after** the code block runs. This guarantees that the code block executes at least once.

dart

```
int attempts = 0;
do {
  print('Attempt number $attempts');
  attempts++;
} while (attempts < 3);
```

o   This loop will execute at least once, even if the condition is initially false.

Real-world Example: Making Decisions in an App

Let's consider a practical example of how control flow can be used in a mobile app: a simple **quiz app** where users answer multiple-choice questions.

Here's how you might handle user answers and control the flow based on their responses:

dart

```
void checkAnswer(String userAnswer) {
  String correctAnswer = "B";

  if (userAnswer == correctAnswer) {
    print("Correct answer!");
  } else {
    print("Wrong answer. Try again!");
  }
}

void main() {
  String userAnswer = 'A'; // Assume the user selected 'A'

  checkAnswer(userAnswer);

  // Implementing a retry mechanism with a loop
  int attempts = 0;
  while (attempts < 3 && userAnswer != "B") {
    print("You have $attempts attempts left.");
    // Simulate user selecting a new answer (we'll assume user enters 'B' after two
wrong attempts)
    userAnswer = attempts == 2 ? 'B' : 'A';
    checkAnswer(userAnswer);
    attempts++;
  }
}
```

Explanation:

- The checkAnswer function checks if the user's answer matches the correct answer.
- A while loop is used to let the user try multiple times (up to 3 attempts), changing the answer on each iteration until they get it right.

This example demonstrates how control flow and loops help make decisions in real-world applications, enhancing user experience by providing feedback and enabling retry mechanisms.

Chapter 6: Functions in Dart

Defining and Calling Functions

In Dart, functions are a fundamental part of programming and allow you to bundle code into reusable blocks. A function can take inputs, process them, and return a result.

Defining Functions: A function in Dart is defined using the void keyword for functions that don't return a value, or the type of the return value (e.g., int, String, etc.) if the function does return something.

dart

```
// Function with no return type (void)
void greet(String name) {
  print('Hello, $name!');
}
```

```
// Function with a return type (String)
String getFullName(String firstName, String lastName) {
  return '$firstName $lastName';
}
```

Calling Functions: Once a function is defined, you can call it by passing the required parameters.

dart

```
void main() {
  greet('John');  // Calling the greet function
  print(getFullName('John', 'Doe'));  // Calling the getFullName function
}
```

Parameters, Return Values, and Function Types

1. **Parameters:** Functions can take zero or more parameters. These parameters can be of any data type, including custom types.

   dart

   ```
   void displayInfo(String name, int age) {
     print('Name: $name, Age: $age');
   }
   ```

   Parameters can also have default values, making them optional when calling the function.

   dart

   ```
   void greet(String name, {String title = 'Mr/Ms'}) {
     print('Hello, $title $name');
   }
   greet('Alice');  // Uses the default value 'Mr/Ms'
   greet('Bob', title: 'Dr');  // Custom value for title
   ```

2. **Return Values:** Functions can return values using the return keyword. The return type of the function is specified before the function name.

dart

```dart
int add(int a, int b) {
  return a + b;
}
```

In this case, the function add takes two integers as input and returns an integer.

3. **Function Types:** Dart allows you to specify types for functions, enabling better code structure and readability. Function types can be used as variable types or parameters.

dart

```dart
// Function type variable
int Function(int, int) addFunc = (int a, int b) => a + b;
print(addFunc(2, 3)); // Output: 5
```

Here, addFunc is a variable that holds a function taking two int parameters and returning an int.

Real-world Example: Building Reusable Functions

Let's say you're building a Flutter app that allows users to create accounts. One of the functionalities is validating user input (e.g., email, password). You can create reusable functions to handle validation logic.

1. **Email Validation Function:**

A reusable function to validate the format of an email address.

dart

```
bool isValidEmail(String email) {
  String pattern = r'^[a-zA-Z0-9._%+-]+@[a-zA-Z0-9.-]+\.[a-zA-Z]{2,}$';
  RegExp regex = RegExp(pattern);
  return regex.hasMatch(email);
}
```

You can now call isValidEmail() whenever you need to check an email's validity in your app.

2. **Password Strength Function:**

A function to check if the password is strong enough (e.g., at least 8 characters, containing both numbers and letters).

dart

```
bool isStrongPassword(String password) {
  RegExp regex = RegExp(r'^(?=.*[0-9])(?=.*[a-zA-Z]).{8,}$');
  return regex.hasMatch(password);
}
```

3. **Using the Functions in the App:**

In your app's user registration logic, you can reuse these functions to ensure the email is valid and the password meets security requirements.

dart

```dart
void registerUser(String email, String password) {
  if (!isValidEmail(email)) {
    print("Invalid email address.");
    return;
  }
  if (!isStrongPassword(password)) {
    print("Password is too weak.");
    return;
  }
  print("Registration successful!");
}
```

This approach allows you to break down your code into small, reusable functions, keeping your app modular, maintainable, and easy to extend.

With this chapter, you'll be comfortable defining functions in Dart, using parameters, returning values, and creating reusable functions for your Flutter app development.

Chapter 7: Widgets in Flutter: The Building Blocks

What are Widgets?

In Flutter, everything is a widget. A widget is a description of part of the user interface, and it defines how an element should look, behave, and interact within an app. It can be anything from a button, text, and image to complex layouts and even entire screens.

Flutter is built around a widget-centric design, meaning the framework's entire UI structure is composed of these small, reusable components. Widgets can be composed hierarchically, with parent widgets containing child widgets to build the full interface. Flutter's declarative approach allows you to simply describe the UI, and the framework takes care of rendering and updating the UI as needed.

For example, a simple text widget is defined as:

dart

```
Text('Hello, Flutter!')
```

In this case, Text is a widget that renders the string "Hello, Flutter!" to the screen.

Stateful vs Stateless Widgets

Flutter defines two types of widgets based on whether or not their state can change:

1. **Stateless**   **Widgets**

   A stateless widget is immutable, meaning once it's created, it cannot change its state or appearance. These widgets only depend on the information passed to them via their constructor.

   Example:

   dart

   ```
   class MyTextWidget extends StatelessWidget {
     final String text;
     MyTextWidget(this.text);

     @override
     Widget build(BuildContext context) {
       return Text(text);
     }
   }
   ```

   o In the example above, MyTextWidget is a stateless widget. It takes text as input and simply displays it. The widget does not change or update after it's created.

2. **Stateful**   **Widgets**

   A stateful widget is dynamic. Its state can change during

the lifecycle of the widget. This type of widget is useful when the UI needs to reflect changes based on user interactions or other events.

Example:

dart

```
class Counter extends StatefulWidget {
  @override
  _CounterState createState() => _CounterState();
}

class _CounterState extends State<Counter> {
  int _counter = 0;

  void _incrementCounter() {
    setState(() {
      _counter++;
    });
  }

  @override
  Widget build(BuildContext context) {
    return Column(
      mainAxisAlignment: MainAxisAlignment.center,
      children: [
        Text('Counter: $_counter'),
        ElevatedButton(
          onPressed: _incrementCounter,
```

```
        child: Text('Increment'),
      ),
    ],
  );
  }
}
```

    o   In the example above, Counter is a stateful widget that maintains and updates its _counter value each time the button is pressed. The setState() method triggers the UI to rebuild with the updated state.

Exploring Flutter's Widget Catalog

Flutter provides an extensive catalog of pre-built widgets, categorized into various types. Here's a brief overview of some key categories:

1. **Basic**   **Widgets**

   These are the core widgets that help you build the basic structure of your app, such as:

       o   Text, Icon, Image

       o   Column, Row, Stack, Container

       o   Padding, Align, Expanded

Example:

dart

```
Container(
  padding: EdgeInsets.all(20),
  color: Colors.blue,
  child: Column(
    children: [
      Text('Hello, Flutter!', style: TextStyle(fontSize: 24)),
      ElevatedButton(onPressed: () {}, child: Text('Press Me'))
    ],
  ),
)
```

2. Input   Widgets

These are widgets that allow users to input data, such as:

- o   TextField, Checkbox, Radio, Switch
- o   Slider, DatePicker, Form

Example:

dart

```
TextField(
  decoration: InputDecoration(
    hintText: 'Enter your name',
  ),
)
```

3. Structural   Widgets

These widgets define the layout of your app, including:

- o   Scaffold, AppBar, Drawer, BottomNavigationBar
- o   ListView, GridView, Stack

Example:

dart

```
Scaffold(
  appBar: AppBar(title: Text('Flutter App')),
  body: Center(child: Text('Welcome to Flutter!')),
)
```

4. **Styling   and   Decoration   Widgets**
These widgets help style your app's UI, including setting colors, borders, shadows, and more.

   o   Container, BoxDecoration, TextStyle, Card, ClipRRect

Example:

dart

```
Container(
  decoration: BoxDecoration(
    color: Colors.green,
    borderRadius: BorderRadius.circular(10),
    boxShadow: [BoxShadow(color: Colors.black26, blurRadius: 5)],
  ),
  child: Text('Styled Box'),
)
```

5. **Animation   Widgets**
Flutter also supports rich animations and transitions:

   o   AnimatedContainer, AnimatedOpacity, FadeTransition

Example:

dart

```
AnimatedContainer(
  duration: Duration(seconds: 1),
  color: _isBlue ? Colors.blue : Colors.red,
  width: _isBig ? 200 : 100,
  height: _isBig ? 200 : 100,
)
```

By leveraging Flutter's diverse widget catalog, you can create complex and beautiful mobile interfaces that remain performant across both iOS and Android devices.

In , understanding how to work with and compose widgets is essential for building robust Flutter apps. Whether you're dealing with simple UI elements or complex layouts, widgets will be your primary building blocks as you develop in Flutter.

Chapter 8: Layouts in Flutter: Organizing the UI

Column, Row, and Stack Widgets

In Flutter, layouts are built using a combination of widgets. The Column, Row, and Stack widgets are essential for structuring the UI and positioning elements vertically, horizontally, or on top of each other.

1. **Column Widget:** The Column widget arranges its children vertically. It takes a list of child widgets and places them in a vertical sequence, one below the other.

   dart

   ```
   Column(
     children: <Widget>[
       Text('First Item'),
       Text('Second Item'),
       ElevatedButton(onPressed: () {}, child: Text('Click Me')),
     ],
   );
   ```

   In this example, the Text widgets and ElevatedButton are stacked vertically.

2. **Row Widget:** The Row widget is the counterpart to Column. It arranges its children horizontally in a left-to-right sequence.

dart

```
Row(
 children: <Widget>[
  Icon(Icons.home),
  Text('Home'),
  Icon(Icons.settings),
 ],
);
```

The Icon and Text widgets are displayed next to each other in a horizontal line.

3. **Stack Widget:** The Stack widget allows children to overlap one another. It positions its children based on the top-left corner of the stack, which allows for layering and more complex designs.

dart

```
Stack(
 children: <Widget>[
  Container(color: Colors.blue, width: 100, height: 100),
  Positioned(
   left: 20,
   top: 20,
```

```
    child: Container(color: Colors.red, width: 50, height: 50),
  ),
 ],
);
```

The Stack widget positions the red square 20 pixels from the top and left of the blue square, creating an overlapping effect.

Understanding Flutter's Layout System

Flutter's layout system is based on a flexible and declarative approach, where the widget tree is the foundation. The key to understanding this system is the concept of ***constraints*** and how Flutter's widgets respond to them.

- **Parent-Child Relationship**: Every widget in Flutter is either a *leaf* widget (that has no children) or a *composite* widget (that contains other widgets). The parent widget gives constraints to its child widgets, dictating the maximum and minimum size the child can occupy.
- **Flex**: The Flex widget, and its subclasses Column and Row, are the backbone of the layout system. These widgets are *flexible*, meaning they can expand and contract based on the available space.
- **Expanded and Flexible**: The Expanded widget tells the parent to give as much space as possible to a child, while

the Flexible widget lets the child take up a portion of the available space, based on a flex factor.

dart

```
Row(
  children: <Widget>[
    Expanded(child: Container(color: Colors.red)),
    Container(color: Colors.blue, width: 50),
    Flexible(child: Container(color: Colors.green)),
  ],
);
```

In this example:

- o The red container expands to take up all remaining horizontal space.
- o The blue container has a fixed width of 50.
- o The green container takes up the remaining space based on its flex factor.

Real-World Example: Designing a Basic App Layout

Let's put these concepts into practice by designing a simple layout for a task list app. We'll use Column, Row, and Stack widgets to build the UI.

Task List App Layout

Here's a simple example of how to build a task list UI:

dart

```dart
import 'package:flutter/material.dart';

void main() {
  runApp(MyApp());
}

class MyApp extends StatelessWidget {
  @override
  Widget build(BuildContext context) {
    return MaterialApp(
      home: TaskListScreen(),
    );
  }
}

class TaskListScreen extends StatelessWidget {
  @override
  Widget build(BuildContext context) {
    return Scaffold(
      appBar: AppBar(title: Text('Task List')),
      body: Column(
        children: [
          // Title Row
          Row(
            mainAxisAlignment: MainAxisAlignment.spaceBetween,
            children: [
              Text('Tasks', style: TextStyle(fontSize: 24)),
              IconButton(
```

```
              icon: Icon(Icons.add),
              onPressed: () {
                // Add task action
              },
            ),
          ],
        ),
        // Task List Column
        Expanded(
          child: ListView(
            children: [
              TaskTile(taskName: 'Buy groceries'),
              TaskTile(taskName: 'Walk the dog'),
              TaskTile(taskName: 'Complete Flutter app'),
            ],
          ),
        ),
      ],
    ),
  );
}
}


class TaskTile extends StatelessWidget {
  final String taskName;

  TaskTile({required this.taskName});

  @override
  Widget build(BuildContext context) {
```

```
  return ListTile(
    leading: Icon(Icons.check_box_outline_blank),
    title: Text(taskName),
    trailing: Icon(Icons.more_vert),
  );
 }
}
```

Explanation:

- **AppBar**: Contains the title "Task List" and an IconButton to add a new task.
- **Row**: The title row is organized horizontally with a Text widget and an IconButton.
- **Expanded**: The ListView is wrapped in an Expanded widget to take up the remaining space in the parent Column.
- **TaskTile**: Each task is represented by a ListTile, which includes a checkbox, the task name, and a more options icon.

In this layout, we've used a combination of Row for horizontal layout, Column for vertical stacking, and ListView for a scrollable list of tasks. This simple structure can be expanded to include more features, such as completing tasks, deleting tasks, or marking tasks as high priority.

By mastering the core layout widgets in Flutter, you can build flexible and responsive UIs for any app, ranging from simple designs to complex, nested structures.

Chapter 9: Handling User Input: Forms, Buttons, and Text Fields

---

TextField, Button, and GestureDetector Widgets

Handling user input is a crucial aspect of mobile app development, and Flutter provides several widgets to collect and process input from users. Among the most commonly used widgets for user interaction are TextField, Button, and GestureDetector.

1. **TextField Widget:**

   The TextField widget allows users to input text. You can customize its behavior, appearance, and validation.

   dart

   ```
   TextField(
     decoration: InputDecoration(
       labelText: 'Enter your name',
       border: OutlineInputBorder(),
     ),
     onChanged: (text) {
       print('User input: $text');
     },
   );
   ```

o   decoration: Allows you to add labels, borders, and other styling to the TextField.

o   onChanged: A callback function triggered whenever the user changes the input.

A TextField can be customized with input formats, error messages, and styles based on the needs of your app.

2. Button Widgets:

Flutter provides several button widgets, such as ElevatedButton, TextButton, and IconButton, to trigger actions when clicked.

dart

```
ElevatedButton(
  onPressed: () {
   print('Button clicked!');
  },
  child: Text('Click Me'),
);
```

o   onPressed: The callback function that is triggered when the button is pressed.

You can easily customize buttons with different styles, colors, and icons.

3. **GestureDetector Widget:**

The GestureDetector widget allows you to detect various gestures such as taps, swipes, and long presses. It's often used to add interactivity to non-button elements.

dart

```
GestureDetector(
 onTap: () {
  print('Tapped!');
 },
 child: Container(
  color: Colors.blue,
  height: 100,
  width: 200,
  child: Center(child: Text('Tap Me')),
 ),
);
```

o   onTap: The callback function triggered when the container is tapped.

This widget is ideal for creating custom interactive areas, such as clickable cards, images, or entire screen regions.

Managing Input Fields

Managing input fields in Flutter is vital for creating user-friendly forms. You often need to validate and store the user input, making sure the form data is in the correct format before submission.

1. **Using Controllers:**

   To manage the text entered in a TextField, Flutter provides a TextEditingController. This allows you to retrieve and modify the text in a TextField.

   dart

   ```
   TextEditingController _controller = TextEditingController();
   ```

   ```
   TextField(
    controller: _controller,
    decoration: InputDecoration(labelText: 'Enter your email'),
   );
   ```
   You can access the value entered by the user like this:

   dart

   ```
   String userInput = _controller.text;
   print(userInput);
   ```

2. **Form Validation:**

   Flutter provides the Form and TextFormField widgets to manage form validation. With these, you can easily validate input fields, show error messages, and handle the form submission.

dart

```
final _formKey = GlobalKey<FormState>();
TextEditingController _emailController = TextEditingController();

Form(
 key: _formKey,
 child: Column(
  children: <Widget>[
   TextFormField(
    controller: _emailController,
    decoration: InputDecoration(labelText: 'Email'),
    validator: (value) {
     if (value == null || value.isEmpty) {
      return 'Please enter an email address';
     }
     return null;
    },
   ),
   ElevatedButton(
    onPressed: () {
     if (_formKey.currentState?.validate() ?? false) {
     // If the form is valid, show a snackbar or submit the data
      print('Form is valid!');
     }
    },
    child: Text('Submit'),
```

```
      ),
    ],
  ),
);
```

- o **GlobalKey<FormState>**: A key used to reference the form for validation.
- o **validator**: A function that checks if the input is valid and returns an error message if necessary.

Real-World Example: Building a Form-Based App

Let's build a simple form for collecting user information such as name and email. This form will include input fields, validation, and a submit button.

dart

```dart
import 'package:flutter/material.dart';

void main() {
  runApp(MyApp());
}

class MyApp extends StatelessWidget {
  @override
  Widget build(BuildContext context) {
    return MaterialApp(
      home: Scaffold(
        appBar: AppBar(title: Text('User Info Form')),
        body: Padding(
```

```
    padding: EdgeInsets.all(16.0),
    child: UserForm(),
  ),
  ),
 );
 }
}


class UserForm extends StatefulWidget {
 @override
 _UserFormState createState() => _UserFormState();
}


class _UserFormState extends State<UserForm> {
 final _formKey = GlobalKey<FormState>();
 final TextEditingController _nameController = TextEditingController();
 final TextEditingController _emailController = TextEditingController();


 @override
 Widget build(BuildContext context) {
  return Form(
   key: _formKey,
   child: Column(
    children: <Widget>[
     TextFormField(
      controller: _nameController,
      decoration: InputDecoration(labelText: 'Name'),
      validator: (value) {
       if (value == null || value.isEmpty) {
        return 'Please enter your name';
```

```
        }
      return null;
      },
    ),
  TextFormField(
    controller: _emailController,
    decoration: InputDecoration(labelText: 'Email'),
    validator: (value) {
      if (value == null || value.isEmpty) {
        return 'Please enter your email';
      }
      if (!RegExp(r'^[^@]+@[^@]+\.[^@]+').hasMatch(value)) {
        return 'Please enter a valid email';
      }
      return null;
      },
    ),
  ElevatedButton(
    onPressed: () {
      if (_formKey.currentState?.validate() ?? false) {
        // If the form is valid, submit data
        ScaffoldMessenger.of(context).showSnackBar(
          SnackBar(content: Text('Submitting data')));
      }
      },
    child: Text('Submit'),
    ),
  ],
  ),
);
```

```
  }
}
```

This code defines a form with two TextFormField widgets for name and email input. Validation ensures the user enters both fields and that the email is in the correct format. The ElevatedButton triggers form submission if the form is valid.

In this chapter, you learned how to handle user input in Flutter using TextField, buttons, and gesture detectors. You also saw how to manage and validate form data, with a real-world example of a user form. With these building blocks, you can start creating interactive and user-friendly forms in your own Flutter applications.

Chapter 10: State Management in Flutter: Basics and Best Practices

---

What is State?

In Flutter, **state** refers to any data or information that can change within the app and affect its behavior or appearance. For example, a button that shows whether it's clicked or not, a counter that increases when tapped, or a form input that changes as the user types—these are all examples of state in Flutter.

State is critical because the app's UI needs to reflect changes in state. Flutter's reactive framework automatically rebuilds the parts of the UI that depend on state changes, which makes it easy to keep the interface in sync with the data.

There are two types of state in Flutter:

- **Ephemeral (local) state**: Temporary state used within a single widget. This can be managed using setState().
- **App-wide (global) state**: More permanent state that needs to be accessed across multiple widgets or screens. This requires a more complex state management solution, like Provider, Riverpod, or BLoC.

Managing State with setState()

setState() is the simplest method of managing state in Flutter. It triggers the rebuild of a widget when its state changes, allowing the UI to reflect those changes.

Here's an example:

dart

```dart
class CounterApp extends StatefulWidget {
  @override
  _CounterAppState createState() => _CounterAppState();
}

class _CounterAppState extends State<CounterApp> {
  int _counter = 0;

  void _incrementCounter() {
    setState(() {
      _counter++; // Changes the state and rebuilds the UI
    });
  }

  @override
  Widget build(BuildContext context) {
    return Scaffold(
      appBar: AppBar(
        title: Text('Counter App'),
      ),
      body: Center(
        child: Column(
```

```
mainAxisAlignment: MainAxisAlignment.center,
children: <Widget>[
  Text(
    'You have pushed the button this many times:',
  ),
  Text(
    '$_counter',
    style: Theme.of(context).textTheme.headline4,
  ),
 ],
),
),
floatingActionButton: FloatingActionButton(
 onPressed: _incrementCounter,
 tooltip: 'Increment',
 child: Icon(Icons.add),
),
);
}
}
```

- **StatefulWidget**: This widget has mutable state, which can change over time.
- **setState()**: This method is called inside the _incrementCounter function. It triggers the rebuild of the widget, updating the UI with the new value of _counter.

Real-World Example: A Counter App with Dynamic State Updates

The counter app is a simple example to demonstrate how state works in Flutter. In this app:

1. The StatefulWidget holds the _counter variable, which is the state of the app.
2. The setState() method updates the value of _counter each time the user taps the button.
3. The UI reflects the new value of _counter, showing dynamic updates.

This app illustrates the core concept of managing local state with setState() in a clean and understandable way, ideal for learning the basics of Flutter state management.

Best Practices for State Management

1. **Use setState() for local state**: For simple, short-lived states (like toggling a button or updating a counter), setState() is sufficient. It keeps the code simple and easy to understand.
2. **Keep state management as local as possible**: Only elevate state to a higher widget (or use external state management solutions) when it becomes too complex to handle with setState() alone.
3. **Avoid excessive rebuilding**: Every time you call setState(), the entire widget tree under that widget will rebuild. Try to

limit the scope of setState() to only the widgets that actually need to update.

4. **Consider more advanced solutions for complex apps**: When building larger apps with more global state (e.g., user authentication or app-wide settings), consider using tools like Provider, Riverpod, or BLoC for more scalable state management.

By following these practices, you can maintain a clean, efficient Flutter application while keeping the codebase easy to manage and debug.

Chapter 11: Navigation and Routing in Flutter

Navigating Between Screens

Navigation allows users to move between different screens or pages in an app. Flutter provides a built-in navigation system to manage routing and transitions between screens.

In Flutter, you use the Navigator widget to manage the stack of screens and the routes between them. Each screen in Flutter is typically represented by a widget, and navigating to a new screen is achieved by pushing that widget onto the navigation stack.

To navigate to a new screen, you use the Navigator.push() method:

dart

```
Navigator.push(
  context,
  MaterialPageRoute(builder: (context) => SecondScreen()),
);
```

- **context**: The current context of the widget, which tells Flutter where in the widget tree the navigation should occur.
- **MaterialPageRoute**: This is a built-in route that provides a material-style transition to the next screen.

- **SecondScreen()**: The screen (or widget) you want to navigate to.

To navigate back to the previous screen, you can use Navigator.pop():

dart

Navigator.pop(context);

This will remove the top screen from the navigation stack and return to the previous one.

Route Names and Route Arguments

In more complex applications, especially with multiple screens, it's often helpful to define routes by name. This makes the navigation cleaner and allows passing arguments between screens.

Defining Named Routes:

First, you define the named routes in the MaterialApp widget:

dart

```
MaterialApp(
  initialRoute: '/',
  routes: {
    '/': (context) => HomeScreen(),
    '/second': (context) => SecondScreen(),
  },
);
```

Now, you can navigate using the route name:

dart

Navigator.pushNamed(context, '/second');

Passing Arguments with Routes:

Sometimes, you need to pass data between screens. You can use the Navigator.pushNamed() method with arguments:

dart

```
Navigator.pushNamed(
  context,
  '/second',
  arguments: 'Hello from HomeScreen!',
);
```

In the target screen, you can retrieve the argument like this:

dart

```
@override
Widget build(BuildContext context) {
  final String message = ModalRoute.of(context)?.settings.arguments as String;
  return Scaffold(
    body: Center(child: Text(message)),
  );
}
```

Real-World Example: Building a Multi-Screen App

Let's build a simple multi-screen app where we navigate from a home screen to a second screen and pass some data.

1. **HomeScreen**: This is the starting point of the app, where the user can click a button to navigate to the second screen.

dart

```
import 'package:flutter/material.dart';

void main() => runApp(MyApp());

class MyApp extends StatelessWidget {
  @override
  Widget build(BuildContext context) {
    return MaterialApp(
      initialRoute: '/',
      routes: {
        '/': (context) => HomeScreen(),
        '/second': (context) => SecondScreen(),
      },
    );
  }
}

class HomeScreen extends StatelessWidget {
  @override
  Widget build(BuildContext context) {
    return Scaffold(
      appBar: AppBar(title: Text('Home Screen')),
      body: Center(
        child: ElevatedButton(
          onPressed: () {
```

```
    Navigator.pushNamed(context, '/second', arguments: 'Hello from Home
Screen!');
      },
      child: Text('Go to Second Screen'),
    ),
   ),
  );
 }
}
```

2. **SecondScreen**: This screen displays the message passed from the HomeScreen.

dart

```
class SecondScreen extends StatelessWidget {
 @override
 Widget build(BuildContext context) {
   final String message = ModalRoute.of(context)?.settings.arguments as String;

   return Scaffold(
     appBar: AppBar(title: Text('Second Screen')),
     body: Center(
       child: Text(message),
     ),
   );
 }
}
```

In this real-world example, we have two screens—HomeScreen and SecondScreen. The user can click a button on the HomeScreen, which navigates to the SecondScreen and passes a message as an argument. The SecondScreen then retrieves and displays the message.

Navigation and routing are fundamental aspects of any mobile app. Flutter's routing system provides an easy-to-use method for managing transitions between screens. Using named routes, passing data between screens, and understanding how the Navigator widget works allows you to create intuitive, multi-screen apps with smooth user experiences.

Chapter 12: Flutter Widgets for User Interaction

Handling Gestures, Taps, Swipes, and Drag Events

User interactions like tapping, swiping, dragging, and other gestures are fundamental in creating an engaging mobile app experience. Flutter provides several widgets and gesture detectors that allow you to capture and respond to these interactions.

1. **Taps and Clicks**:

   The most common form of user interaction is tapping or clicking. You can handle this with widgets like GestureDetector, InkWell, and FlatButton (or ElevatedButton in more recent versions).

   Example: A button that responds to a tap:

   dart

```
GestureDetector(
  onTap: () {
    print("Tapped!");
  },
  child: Container(
    padding: EdgeInsets.all(10),
```

```
color: Colors.blue,
  child: Text("Tap Me", style: TextStyle(color: Colors.white)),
 ),
);
```

In this case, the GestureDetector captures the tap gesture, and the onTap callback is triggered when the user taps the container.

2. **Swipes**:

Swiping gestures (e.g., left, right, up, down) are often used in apps for tasks like navigating between pages or deleting items from a list.

Example: Detecting a swipe gesture:

dart

```
GestureDetector(
  onHorizontalDragUpdate: (details) {
    if (details.primaryDelta! > 0) {
      print("Swiped Right");
    } else {
      print("Swiped Left");
    }
  },
  child: Container(
    color: Colors.green,
    child: Text("Swipe Me", style: TextStyle(color: Colors.white)),
  ),
```

);

The onHorizontalDragUpdate callback is triggered during a horizontal drag, and details.primaryDelta provides information on the direction of the swipe.

3. **Drag Events**:

Dragging is often used for interacting with elements that the user can move around the screen, such as dragging items in a list or dragging a slider.

Example: Detecting a drag gesture:

dart

```
GestureDetector(
  onPanUpdate: (details) {
   print("Dragging: ${details.localPosition}");
  },
  child: Container(
   color: Colors.orange,
   height: 100,
   width: 100,
   child: Center(child: Text("Drag Me")),
  ),
);
```

The onPanUpdate callback tracks the position of the drag and can be used to move an element across the screen or update its state.

Flutter's GestureDetector and Other Input Widgets

- **GestureDetector**: A versatile widget that allows you to capture various types of gestures, including taps, double taps, long presses, swipes, and more. It is highly customizable and can be used with almost any child widget.

- **InkWell**: An interactive widget that provides a ripple effect when tapped, mimicking the material design interaction style. It is typically used for buttons or clickable areas.

Example:

dart

```
InkWell(
  onTap: () {
    print("InkWell tapped!");
  },
  child: Container(
    padding: EdgeInsets.all(10),
    color: Colors.purple,
    child: Text("Click Me", style: TextStyle(color: Colors.white)),
  ),
);
```

- **FlatButton, ElevatedButton, and IconButton**: Buttons are key interactive elements in Flutter. These buttons can be customized with callbacks, colors, icons, and text to fit the app's needs.

Real-World Example: Interactive Elements in Your App

Imagine building a simple app that allows users to "like" or "dislike" a post by tapping a button. You can use Flutter's gesture detection to handle the tap events and update the UI accordingly.

dart

```dart
class LikeDislikeApp extends StatefulWidget {
 @override
 _LikeDislikeAppState createState() => _LikeDislikeAppState();
}

class _LikeDislikeAppState extends State<LikeDislikeApp> {
 int likes = 0;
 int dislikes = 0;

 void _incrementLikes() {
  setState(() {
   likes++;
  });
 }

 void _incrementDislikes() {
  setState(() {
   dislikes++;
  });
 }

 @override
 Widget build(BuildContext context) {
```

```dart
    return Scaffold(
      appBar: AppBar(title: Text("Interactive Like/Dislike")),
      body: Center(
        child: Column(
          mainAxisAlignment: MainAxisAlignment.center,
          children: [
            GestureDetector(
              onTap: _incrementLikes,
              child: Container(
                padding: EdgeInsets.all(20),
                color: Colors.green,
                child: Text('Like: $likes', style: TextStyle(color: Colors.white)),
              ),
            ),
            SizedBox(height: 20),
            GestureDetector(
              onTap: _incrementDislikes,
              child: Container(
                padding: EdgeInsets.all(20),
                color: Colors.red,
                child: Text('Dislike: $dislikes', style: TextStyle(color: Colors.white)),
              ),
            ),
          ],
        ),
      ),
    );
  }
}
```

In this real-world example:

- Two GestureDetector widgets are used to handle taps on the like and dislike buttons.
- When a user taps a button, the corresponding value (likes or dislikes) is incremented and updated in the UI using setState().

This approach allows users to interact with elements in real-time, and you can build on this to create more complex interactive features, such as swiping between posts or dragging items to reorder them.

This chapter covers the basics of handling user input in Flutter through gestures and interactive widgets, equipping you with the tools to build engaging and dynamic apps.

Chapter 13: Working with Lists and Grids in Flutter

ListView and GridView Widgets

In Flutter, displaying large collections of data, such as lists or grids, is a common task. The ListView and GridView widgets provide efficient and flexible ways to display dynamic collections of items. Both widgets support scrolling, and they handle rendering only the visible items to optimize performance when working with large data sets.

1. **ListView Widget:**

   ListView is a scrollable list of widgets that is commonly used for displaying vertical lists. It can be constructed in several ways, depending on the data structure and requirements.

   o **Basic ListView:**

   dart

```
ListView(
  children: <Widget>[
    ListTile(title: Text("Item 1")),
```

```
    ListTile(title: Text("Item 2")),
    ListTile(title: Text("Item 3")),
  ],
);
```

○ **ListView.builder**: This is used when you need to display a large, dynamic list. It builds the widgets lazily as the user scrolls.

dart

```
ListView.builder(
  itemCount: items.length,
  itemBuilder: (context, index) {
    return ListTile(
      title: Text(items[index]),
    );
  },
);
```

The ListView.builder is especially useful for long lists, as it only builds the widgets that are visible on the screen, improving performance.

2. **GridView Widget:**

GridView is similar to ListView but arranges items in a 2D grid. This is perfect for displaying data in a matrix, such as images or product catalogs.

o **Basic GridView:**

dart

```
GridView(
  gridDelegate: SliverGridDelegateWithFixedCrossAxisCount(
    crossAxisCount: 2, // Number of columns
    crossAxisSpacing: 10, // Horizontal spacing between items
    mainAxisSpacing: 10,  // Vertical spacing between items
  ),
  children: <Widget>[
    Container(color: Colors.blue, child: Text("Item 1")),
    Container(color: Colors.green, child: Text("Item 2")),
    Container(color: Colors.orange, child: Text("Item 3")),
  ],
);
```

o **GridView.builder**: Similar to ListView.builder, GridView.builder builds only the visible items, making it highly efficient for large grids.

dart

```
GridView.builder(
  gridDelegate: SliverGridDelegateWithFixedCrossAxisCount(
    crossAxisCount: 3,
    crossAxisSpacing: 10,
    mainAxisSpacing: 10,
  ),
  itemCount: productList.length,
```

```
itemBuilder: (context, index) {
  return GridTile(
    child: Image.network(productList[index].imageUrl),
  );
},
);
```

Handling Long Lists and Grids of Data

Working with long lists and grids in Flutter requires efficient rendering to avoid performance bottlenecks. Both ListView and GridView widgets support lazy loading, which means they only build the widgets that are visible to the user. This can be further optimized with techniques like:

1. **Caching Data**: For large data sets, consider caching items that the user has already scrolled past, so they don't need to be rebuilt each time they reappear.

2. **Pagination and Infinite Scrolling**: For lists or grids with a large number of items, you can implement infinite scrolling by fetching more data as the user scrolls to the end.

   Example of infinite scrolling:

   dart

   ```
   ScrollController _scrollController = ScrollController();

   @override
   void initState() {
   ```

```dart
    super.initState();
    _scrollController.addListener(() {
      if          (_scrollController.position.pixels          ==
    _scrollController.position.maxScrollExtent) {
        // Fetch more data when the user reaches the bottom
        fetchMoreData();
      }
    });
  }

  @override
  Widget build(BuildContext context) {
    return ListView.builder(
      controller: _scrollController,
      itemCount: items.length,
      itemBuilder: (context, index) {
        return ListTile(title: Text(items[index]));
      },
    );
  }
```

Real-World Example: Building a Product Listing Screen

Let's say you want to create a product listing screen, like an e-commerce app, that displays products in a grid.

dart

```dart
class Product {
  final String name;
  final String imageUrl;
  final double price;
```

```
Product({required this.name, required this.imageUrl, required this.price});
}


class ProductListingScreen extends StatelessWidget {
  final List<Product> products = [
    Product(name: "Product 1", imageUrl: "url1", price: 10.99),
    Product(name: "Product 2", imageUrl: "url2", price: 20.99),
    Product(name: "Product 3", imageUrl: "url3", price: 15.49),
    // More products
  ];


  @override
  Widget build(BuildContext context) {
    return Scaffold(
      appBar: AppBar(title: Text("Product Listing")),
      body: GridView.builder(
        gridDelegate: SliverGridDelegateWithFixedCrossAxisCount(
          crossAxisCount: 2,
          crossAxisSpacing: 8.0,
          mainAxisSpacing: 8.0,
        ),
        itemCount: products.length,
        itemBuilder: (context, index) {
          final product = products[index];
          return Card(
            child: Column(
              children: [
                Image.network(product.imageUrl, height: 100, width: 100),
                Text(product.name),
```

```
        Text("\$${product.price}"),
      ],
     ),
   );
  },
 ),
);
 }
}
```

In this example:

- We create a Product class with properties like name, imageUrl, and price.
- The ProductListingScreen uses a GridView.builder to display products in a 2-column grid.
- Each product is displayed with an image, name, and price.

This screen is optimized for dynamic data, and you can easily expand it to load data from an API or local storage.

By the end of this chapter, you should be comfortable with using ListView and GridView widgets to display dynamic collections of data, as well as handling performance optimizations like lazy loading and infinite scrolling.

Chapter 14: **Asynchronous Programming with Dart and Flutter**

Future, async, await, and Streams

Asynchronous programming is crucial in modern mobile app development because it allows apps to remain responsive while performing tasks that take time, such as fetching data from a server, reading files, or making network requests. Dart and Flutter provide powerful tools for handling asynchronous operations, including Future, async, await, and Stream.

1. **Future**:

   A Future represents a value that will be available at some point in the future, after an asynchronous operation completes. It can either complete with a result (success) or with an error (failure).

   Example of using a Future:

   dart

   ```
   Future<String> fetchData() async {
     await Future.delayed(Duration(seconds: 2));  // Simulate delay
     return 'Data fetched successfully';
   }
   ```

2. **async and await**:

   o **async**: Marks a function as asynchronous, allowing you to use await within it.

   o **await**: Pauses execution of the function until the Future completes, without blocking the entire program.

Example of using async and await:

dart

```
void getData() async {
  String result = await fetchData();  // Wait for the Future to complete
  print(result);  // Prints: Data fetched successfully
}
```

In this example, await waits for the fetchData Future to complete before continuing with the rest of the code.

3. **Streams**:

While a Future represents a single value that will be available later, a Stream represents a sequence of asynchronous events. You can use streams to listen for multiple values over time (e.g., data coming in from a network, user input events, etc.).

Example of using a Stream:

dart

```
Stream<int> countStream() async* {
  for (int i = 0; i < 5; i++) {
    await Future.delayed(Duration(seconds: 1));
    yield i;
  }
}
```

This stream will yield values (0 to 4) with a 1-second delay between each.

Handling Async Tasks like API Calls and File I/O

Asynchronous programming is especially useful for tasks like API calls, network requests, and file I/O, which can take time to complete but shouldn't block the main thread. In Flutter, you commonly use http for making API requests and dart:io for handling files.

1. **Making API Calls with http**:

   To fetch data from a remote server, you can use the http package. This package provides an easy way to make HTTP requests and handle responses asynchronously.

   Example of fetching data from an API:

   dart

   ```
   import 'package:http/http.dart' as http;
   ```

```dart
Future<void> fetchDataFromAPI() async {
  final response = await
http.get(Uri.parse('https://jsonplaceholder.typicode.com/posts'));
  if (response.statusCode == 200) {
    print('Data: ${response.body}');
  } else {
    throw Exception('Failed to load data');
  }
}
```

- o In this example, we send a GET request to an API and print the response body if the status code is 200 OK.

2. **Handling File I/O**:

Reading from and writing to files is another common use case for async programming. Dart's dart:io library provides classes like File to handle file operations.

Example of reading a file asynchronously:

dart

```dart
import 'dart:io';

Future<void> readFile() async {
  final file = File('path_to_your_file.txt');
  String contents = await file.readAsString();
  print(contents);
```

}

- o This code reads the contents of a file asynchronously and prints it to the console.

Real-World Example: Fetching and Displaying Data from a Remote Server

Now, let's bring everything together with a real-world example: fetching data from a remote server and displaying it in your app. We will fetch a list of posts from a mock API and display them in a ListView.

1. **Dependencies**: Add the http package to your pubspec.yaml file:

yaml

```
dependencies:
  flutter:
    sdk: flutter
  http: ^0.13.4
```

2. **Fetching Data from the API**:

Create a model to store the data (Post) and a function to fetch the posts.

```dart
import 'dart:convert';
import 'package:flutter/material.dart';
import 'package:http/http.dart' as http;

class Post {
  final int id;
  final String title;
  final String body;

  Post({required this.id, required this.title, required this.body});

  factory Post.fromJson(Map<String, dynamic> json) {
    return Post(
      id: json['id'],
      title: json['title'],
      body: json['body'],
    );
  }
}

Future<List<Post>> fetchPosts() async {
  final response = await
http.get(Uri.parse('https://jsonplaceholder.typicode.com/posts'));
  if (response.statusCode == 200) {
    List<dynamic> data = json.decode(response.body);
    return data.map((json) => Post.fromJson(json)).toList();
  } else {
    throw Exception('Failed to load posts');
```

```
    }
  }
```

3. Displaying Data in the UI:

Now, we can display the fetched posts in a ListView.

dart

```
class PostListScreen extends StatelessWidget {
 @override
 Widget build(BuildContext context) {
  return Scaffold(
    appBar: AppBar(
     title: Text('Posts'),
    ),
    body: FutureBuilder<List<Post>>(
     future: fetchPosts(),
     builder: (context, snapshot) {
      if (snapshot.connectionState == ConnectionState.waiting) {
       return Center(child: CircularProgressIndicator());
      } else if (snapshot.hasError) {
       return Center(child: Text('Error: ${snapshot.error}'));
      } else if (!snapshot.hasData) {
       return Center(child: Text('No posts available'));
      } else {
       List<Post> posts = snapshot.data!;
       return ListView.builder(
         itemCount: posts.length,
         itemBuilder: (context, index) {
          return ListTile(
```

```
                title: Text(posts[index].title),
                subtitle: Text(posts[index].body),
              );
            },
          );
        }
      },
    ),
  );
}
}
```

```
void main() => runApp(MaterialApp(home: PostListScreen()));
```

In this example:

- **FutureBuilder** is used to asynchronously fetch and display the data.
- The ListView.builder creates a scrollable list of posts fetched from the remote server.

By using async, await, and handling asynchronous tasks like API calls, your Flutter app can remain responsive while interacting with external data sources and performing time-consuming tasks.

Chapter 15: Integrating APIs into Your Flutter App

HTTP Requests in Flutter

One of the core features of modern mobile applications is the ability to interact with external APIs to fetch, send, or modify data. Flutter provides a simple way to make HTTP requests using the http package, which allows you to communicate with RESTful APIs, perform GET/POST requests, and handle responses.

To get started with HTTP requests in Flutter, you need to add the http package to your pubspec.yaml file:

yaml

```
dependencies:
 flutter:
  sdk: flutter
 http: ^0.13.3  # Add this line for HTTP functionality
```

Then, you can use it to make API calls. Here's an example of making a simple GET request:

dart

```
import 'package:http/http.dart' as http;
import 'dart:convert';  // For parsing JSON data
```

```
Future<void> fetchData() async {
  final response = await http.get(Uri.parse('https://api.example.com/data'));

  if (response.statusCode == 200) {
    // If the server returns a 200 OK response, parse the JSON
    var data = json.decode(response.body);
    print(data);  // Use the parsed data
  } else {
    // If the server returns an error, throw an exception
    throw Exception('Failed to load data');
  }
}
```

In this example:

- http.get() is used to make a GET request to the provided URL.
- If the request is successful (status code 200), the response body is parsed from JSON format using json.decode().
- If the request fails, an exception is thrown.

Parsing JSON Data

JSON (JavaScript Object Notation) is the most common format used by web APIs to exchange data. Dart's dart:convert library makes it easy to parse JSON data into Dart objects and vice versa.

Here's how you can parse JSON data into a Dart model class:

1. **Create a Dart model class** to represent the structure of the data:

dart

```dart
class Weather {
  final String city;
  final double temperature;

  Weather({required this.city, required this.temperature});

  factory Weather.fromJson(Map<String, dynamic> json) {
    return Weather(
      city: json['city'],
      temperature: json['temperature'].toDouble(),
    );
  }
}
```

2. Parse the JSON response into the model class:

dart

```dart
Future<Weather> fetchWeather() async {
  final response = await http.get(Uri.parse('https://api.weather.com/data'));

  if (response.statusCode == 200) {
    var jsonData = json.decode(response.body);
    return Weather.fromJson(jsonData);
  } else {
    throw Exception('Failed to load weather data');
  }
```

```
}
```

- o The Weather.fromJson() method converts the raw JSON map into a Dart object (Weather), making it easier to work with the data.

Real-World Example: Fetching Weather Data from an API

Now, let's put everything together to create a real-world example: a simple Flutter app that fetches weather data from an API and displays it on the screen.

1. **Add the necessary dependencies** (in pubspec.yaml):

yaml

```yaml
dependencies:
  flutter:
    sdk: flutter
  http: ^0.13.3
```

2. **Create the Weather model class** as shown above.
3. **Create the app with a simple UI** to display the weather data.

dart

```dart
import 'package:flutter/material.dart';
import 'package:http/http.dart' as http;
import 'dart:convert';
```

```
class Weather {
  final String city;
  final double temperature;

  Weather({required this.city, required this.temperature});

  factory Weather.fromJson(Map<String, dynamic> json) {
    return Weather(
      city: json['city'],
      temperature: json['temperature'].toDouble(),
    );
  }
}

void main() {
  runApp(MyApp());
}

class MyApp extends StatelessWidget {
  @override
  Widget build(BuildContext context) {
    return MaterialApp(
      title: 'Weather App',
      home: WeatherScreen(),
    );
  }
}

class WeatherScreen extends StatefulWidget {
```

```
  @override
  _WeatherScreenState createState() => _WeatherScreenState();
}


class _WeatherScreenState extends State<WeatherScreen> {
  late Future<Weather> futureWeather;

  @override
  void initState() {
    super.initState();
    futureWeather = fetchWeather();
  }

  Future<Weather> fetchWeather() async {
    final             response             =             await
http.get(Uri.parse('https://api.weather.com/data'));

    if (response.statusCode == 200) {
      var jsonData = json.decode(response.body);
      return Weather.fromJson(jsonData);
    } else {
      throw Exception('Failed to load weather data');
    }
  }

  @override
  Widget build(BuildContext context) {
    return Scaffold(
      appBar: AppBar(
        title: Text('Weather App'),
```

```
        ),
      body: Center(
        child: FutureBuilder<Weather>(
          future: futureWeather,
          builder: (context, snapshot) {
            if (snapshot.connectionState == ConnectionState.waiting) {
              return CircularProgressIndicator();
            } else if (snapshot.hasError) {
              return Text('Error: ${snapshot.error}');
            } else if (snapshot.hasData) {
              Weather weather = snapshot.data!;
              return Column(
                mainAxisAlignment: MainAxisAlignment.center,
                children: [
                  Text('City: ${weather.city}', style: TextStyle(fontSize: 24)),
                  Text('Temperature:    ${weather.temperature}°C',    style:
TextStyle(fontSize: 24)),
                ],
              );
            } else {
              return Text('No data available');
            }
          },
        ),
      ),
    );
  }
}
```

Explanation:

- **Model class**: The Weather class models the data returned by the weather API.

- **Fetching data**: fetchWeather() makes an HTTP GET request to the weather API and parses the response into a Weather object.

- **UI**: The WeatherScreen widget fetches the data asynchronously using a FutureBuilder. The UI updates based on the state of the Future (waiting, error, or data).

In this example, we simulate fetching weather data from an API, display the result in a simple UI, and handle potential errors effectively.

This approach can be applied to any API you want to integrate into your Flutter app, whether it's for weather, news, e-commerce, or any other service.

Chapter 16: Persistent Storage: Saving Data in Flutter

SharedPreferences, SQLite, and Firebase

When building mobile apps, there's often a need to persist data between app sessions. Flutter offers several options for storing data, ranging from simple key-value storage to more complex relational databases and cloud-based solutions.

1. **SharedPreferences:**

   SharedPreferences is a simple key-value storage system that allows you to store primitive data types like strings, integers, and booleans. It's perfect for saving small amounts of data, such as user preferences or simple settings.

   To use SharedPreferences, add the following dependency to your pubspec.yaml:

   yaml

   dependencies:
     shared_preferences: ^2.0.15

   Example of using SharedPreferences to save and retrieve data:

   dart

```
import 'package:shared_preferences/shared_preferences.dart';

// Save a preference
Future<void> savePreference(String key, String value) async {
  final prefs = await SharedPreferences.getInstance();
  await prefs.setString(key, value);
}

// Retrieve a preference
Future<String?> getPreference(String key) async {
  final prefs = await SharedPreferences.getInstance();
  return prefs.getString(key);
}
```

This method allows you to store data locally for quick access, such as a user's theme choice or language setting.

2. **SQLite:**

For more complex data storage needs, such as saving structured data, SQLite is a powerful option. Flutter provides a package called sqflite to work with SQLite databases.

To add SQLite support, include the sqflite package in your pubspec.yaml:

yaml

dependencies:

sqflite: ^2.0.0+4

Example of using SQLite to store and retrieve a list of users:

dart

```dart
import 'package:sqflite/sqflite.dart';
import 'package:path/path.dart';

// Initialize database
Future<Database> initDB() async {
  var dbPath = await getDatabasesPath();
  return openDatabase(join(dbPath, 'user_db.db'),
    onCreate: (db, version) async {
      await db.execute(
        'CREATE TABLE Users(id INTEGER PRIMARY KEY, name TEXT)',
      );
    }, version: 1);
}

// Insert a user
Future<void> insertUser(Database db, String name) async {
  await db.insert('Users', {'name': name});
}

// Retrieve users
Future<List<Map<String, dynamic>>> fetchUsers(Database db) async {
  return await db.query('Users');
}
```

SQLite is ideal for storing complex models, like lists of items or user-generated data, that need to be queried and updated.

3. **Firebase:**

For cloud-based persistent storage, Firebase provides a comprehensive solution. Firebase offers services like **Firestore** (NoSQL database) and **Firebase Realtime Database** to sync data across devices in real-time.

To use Firebase, you need to add the firebase_core and cloud_firestore packages to your pubspec.yaml:

yaml

```
dependencies:
  firebase_core: ^1.10.6
  cloud_firestore: ^3.1.5
```

Example of storing and retrieving data using Firestore:

dart

```
import 'package:cloud_firestore/cloud_firestore.dart';

// Save a user to Firestore
Future<void> saveUser() async {
  FirebaseFirestore.instance.collection('users').add({
    'name': 'John Doe',
    'email': 'johndoe@example.com',
```

```
  });
}
```

```
// Retrieve users from Firestore
Future<void> getUsers() async {
  var          snapshot          =          await
FirebaseFirestore.instance.collection('users').get();
  for (var doc in snapshot.docs) {
    print(doc.data());
  }
}
```

Firebase is ideal for real-time data synchronization across multiple devices or users and is a great choice for apps that need cloud storage and online syncing.

Storing Simple Data and Complex Models

1. **Storing Simple Data**: Simple data, such as user settings, preferences, or flags, can be easily stored using SharedPreferences or SQLite. These are best for small, key-value pairs or simple records.

2. **Storing Complex Models**: When dealing with more complex data structures, like lists or models with nested objects, SQLite or Firebase is preferred. You can serialize complex models into JSON before storing them or use relational databases for better querying capabilities.

For example, in SQLite, you would create a model class and convert it to a map before saving it:

dart

```
class User {
  final int id;
  final String name;

  User({required this.id, required this.name});

  Map<String, dynamic> toMap() {
    return {'id': id, 'name': name};
  }
}
```

Similarly, when using Firebase, you can store a complex model as a map:

dart

```
FirebaseFirestore.instance.collection('users').add({
  'id': user.id,
  'name': user.name,
});
```

Real-World Example: Storing User Preferences Locally

Consider an app that allows the user to choose between a light or dark theme. You can use SharedPreferences to store the theme setting so that the app remembers the user's choice across sessions.

dart

```dart
import 'package:flutter/material.dart';
import 'package:shared_preferences/shared_preferences.dart';

void main() {
  runApp(MyApp());
}

class MyApp extends StatefulWidget {
  @override
  _MyAppState createState() => _MyAppState();
}

class _MyAppState extends State<MyApp> {
  bool isDarkMode = false;

  @override
  void initState() {
    super.initState();
    _loadThemePreference();
  }

  // Load theme preference from SharedPreferences
  _loadThemePreference() async {
    final prefs = await SharedPreferences.getInstance();
    setState(() {
      isDarkMode = prefs.getBool('isDarkMode') ?? false;
    });
  }
```

```dart
// Save theme preference
_saveThemePreference(bool value) async {
  final prefs = await SharedPreferences.getInstance();
  prefs.setBool('isDarkMode', value);
}


@override
Widget build(BuildContext context) {
  return MaterialApp(
    themeMode: isDarkMode ? ThemeMode.dark : ThemeMode.light,
    darkTheme: ThemeData.dark(),
    theme: ThemeData.light(),
    home: Scaffold(
      appBar: AppBar(title: Text('Theme Preferences')),
      body: Center(
        child: Switch(
          value: isDarkMode,
          onChanged: (value) {
            setState(() {
              isDarkMode = value;
            });
            _saveThemePreference(value);
          },
        ),
      ),
    ),
  );
}
}
```

In this example:

- The app stores the user's theme preference in SharedPreferences and remembers it between app launches.
- The Switch widget allows the user to toggle between light and dark themes, and the preference is saved and loaded when the app starts.

:

By leveraging tools like SharedPreferences, SQLite, and Firebase, Flutter allows you to handle both simple and complex persistent storage needs. Whether you need to store user settings, offline data, or synchronize data across devices, you can choose the right storage solution for your app's requirements.

Chapter 17: Working with Databases: SQLite and Firebase

Introduction to SQLite in Flutter

SQLite is a powerful, lightweight, serverless database engine used for storing structured data locally on mobile devices. It's commonly used in Flutter apps for storing data offline, such as user preferences, app settings, or other small datasets that need to be queried efficiently.

To use SQLite in Flutter, you can use the sqflite package, which provides a wrapper around SQLite and allows you to perform CRUD (Create, Read, Update, Delete) operations.

Setting up SQLite:

First, add the sqflite and path packages to your pubspec.yaml file:

yaml

```
dependencies:
  sqflite: ^2.0.0+4
  path: ^1.8.0
```

To create a simple SQLite database:

dart

```
import 'package:sqflite/sqflite.dart';
import 'package:path/path.dart';

// Open or create the database
Future<Database> openDatabaseConnection() async {
  final dbPath = await getDatabasesPath();
  return openDatabase(
    join(dbPath, 'todo.db'),
    onCreate: (db, version) {
      return db.execute(
        'CREATE TABLE todos(id INTEGER PRIMARY KEY, title TEXT)',
      );
    },
    version: 1,
  );
}

// Insert data into the database
Future<void> insertTodo(Database db, String title) async {
  await db.insert(
    'todos',
    {'title': title},
    conflictAlgorithm: ConflictAlgorithm.replace,
  );
}

// Fetch data from the database
Future<List<Map<String, dynamic>>> fetchTodos(Database db) async {
  return await db.query('todos');
}
```

This basic example demonstrates creating a table and performing basic operations like inserting and fetching to-do items. You can expand this to add more complex models or relationships between data.

Using Firebase as a Backend

Firebase is a cloud-based platform by Google that offers a comprehensive suite of tools and services for mobile app development, including real-time databases, authentication, cloud functions, and more. Firebase is often used as a backend solution for storing and syncing data between devices and cloud storage.

To use Firebase in your Flutter app, you'll need to set up Firebase by adding it to your project and integrating the relevant Firebase packages. For example, for using Firebase Firestore (a NoSQL database) for storing and retrieving data, add the following dependencies:

yaml

```
dependencies:
  firebase_core: ^1.10.0
  cloud_firestore: ^3.1.5
```

Firebase Setup:

1. Initialize Firebase in your app:

dart

```dart
import 'package:firebase_core/firebase_core.dart';

void main() async {
  WidgetsFlutterBinding.ensureInitialized();
  await Firebase.initializeApp();
  runApp(MyApp());
}
```

2. Interact with Firebase Firestore to add, read, or update data:

dart

```dart
import 'package:cloud_firestore/cloud_firestore.dart';

// Add a new to-do item
Future<void> addTodoToFirebase(String title) async {
  await FirebaseFirestore.instance.collection('todos').add({
    'title': title,
    'created_at': FieldValue.serverTimestamp(),
  });
}

// Fetch to-do items from Firestore
Future<List<Map<String, dynamic>>> fetchTodosFromFirebase()
async {
  QuerySnapshot snapshot = await FirebaseFirestore.instance
      .collection('todos')
      .orderBy('created_at')
      .get();
```

```
    return snapshot.docs.map((doc) {
     return {'id': doc.id, 'title': doc['title']};
    }).toList();
   }
```

Firebase handles real-time syncing, which means data changes made on one device are immediately reflected across all devices connected to the same Firebase project.

Real-World Example: A To-Do List App with Local and Cloud Storage

Combining SQLite and Firebase can be extremely useful when you need to handle both local and cloud-based storage in your app. In this example, we'll build a simple to-do list app that stores tasks locally using SQLite and syncs them with Firebase for cloud storage.

1. **Local Storage with SQLite:** Use SQLite to store to-do items locally on the device for offline access.

2. **Syncing Data with Firebase:** Sync new tasks with Firebase when the device is online, allowing the data to be available across all user devices.

Example Workflow:

- When a user adds a new to-do item, the app saves it to the local SQLite database first.

- If the device is online, the app then pushes the new to-do item to Firebase.

- When the app starts, it loads the to-do items from the SQLite database. If the app detects that there are new items on Firebase (such as from another device), it can sync those changes.

dart

```dart
import 'package:sqflite/sqflite.dart';
import 'package:cloud_firestore/cloud_firestore.dart';

// Save to Firebase if online
Future<void> syncTodoToFirebase(Database db) async {
  List<Map<String, dynamic>> todos = await fetchTodos(db);

  for (var todo in todos) {
    // Push each todo to Firebase if not already synced
    FirebaseFirestore.instance.collection('todos').add(todo);
  }
}

// Sync from Firebase
Future<void> syncFromFirebaseToLocal(Database db) async {
  QuerySnapshot snapshot = await
FirebaseFirestore.instance.collection('todos').get();

  for (var doc in snapshot.docs) {
    Map<String, dynamic> todoData = doc.data();
```

```
  insertTodo(db, todoData['title']);  // Save to local SQLite database
 }
}
```

By integrating SQLite for local storage and Firebase for cloud storage, this to-do app provides offline functionality with seamless syncing to the cloud when the device is online. This approach ensures that users have a smooth experience regardless of connectivity status.

This chapter covers the basics of working with databases in Flutter, from using SQLite for local storage to integrating Firebase for cloud-based data management. With both solutions, you can store and sync data effectively, whether offline or online.

Chapter 18: **Building and Using Flutter Packages**

Exploring the Flutter Package Ecosystem

The Flutter ecosystem has a vast collection of open-source packages available through **pub.dev**, Flutter's package manager, which is the go-to place for developers to share libraries and tools. These packages simplify common tasks, from adding third-party integrations (e.g., Google Maps, Firebase) to enhancing your app's UI with animations and custom widgets.

Flutter's package ecosystem is continually evolving, and it's an essential part of building high-quality apps without reinventing the wheel. By leveraging these packages, you can focus on building the unique aspects of your app while using pre-built solutions for common functionalities.

Some popular categories of packages include:

- **Networking**: HTTP requests, WebSocket communication, GraphQL clients.
- **Database**: SQLite, Firebase, Realm, Moor.
- **UI**: Custom animations, material design components, icons.
- **Integration**: Google Maps, Facebook Login, Stripe, Firebase, etc.

Example of using a package: Let's look at integrating Google Maps into your Flutter app.

How to Find and Use Packages

To find and use packages in your Flutter app, follow these steps:

1. **Search for a Package on pub.dev:** Visit pub.dev and search for a package that fits your needs. For example, searching for "google_maps_flutter" will show the official Google Maps package for Flutter.

2. **Add the Package to pubspec.yaml:**

   Once you've found the package, add it to your project's pubspec.yaml file under the dependencies section.

   yaml

   ```
   dependencies:
    google_maps_flutter: ^2.1.1  # Use the latest stable version
   ```

3. **Install the Package:** Run flutter pub get in your terminal to download and install the package.

4. **Import the Package into Your Code:** After installation, you can import the package into your Dart file and begin using it.

   dart

   ```
   import 'package:google_maps_flutter/google_maps_flutter.dart';
   ```

Real-World Example: Integrating Google Maps or Other Packages

In this example, we'll integrate the **Google Maps** package into a Flutter app to display a map and add a marker.

1. **Setup:**
   - Make sure you've followed the necessary setup steps for **Google Maps API** in both Android and iOS (for Google Maps integration). This includes adding the necessary API keys to your Android and iOS project files.

2. **Code Example**:

   Here's how you can create a simple Google Map with a marker:

   dart

   ```
   import 'package:flutter/material.dart';
   import 'package:google_maps_flutter/google_maps_flutter.dart';

   class MapScreen extends StatefulWidget {
    @override
    _MapScreenState createState() => _MapScreenState();
   }

   class _MapScreenState extends State<MapScreen> {
    GoogleMapController? _mapController;
   ```

```
// Define initial camera position
final CameraPosition _initialPosition = CameraPosition(
  target: LatLng(37.7749, -122.4194),    // Coordinates for San Francisco
  zoom: 12,
);

// Define a marker
final Marker _marker = Marker(
  markerId: MarkerId('marker_1'),
  position: LatLng(37.7749, -122.4194),
  infoWindow: InfoWindow(title: 'San Francisco'),
);

@override
Widget build(BuildContext context) {
  return Scaffold(
    appBar: AppBar(
      title: Text('Google Maps in Flutter'),
    ),
    body: GoogleMap(
      initialCameraPosition: _initialPosition,
      markers: {_marker},
      onMapCreated: (GoogleMapController controller) {
        _mapController = controller;
      },
    ),
  );
}
}
```

```
void main() {
 runApp(MaterialApp(
  home: MapScreen(),
 ));
}
```

Explanation:

- o GoogleMap widget: Displays the map.
- o initialCameraPosition: Sets the initial position and zoom level of the map.
- o Marker: Adds a marker at the given location.
- o onMapCreated: Gets called when the map is fully initialized, giving you a reference to the GoogleMapController, which you can use to control the map (like moving the camera).

3. **Run the App:** Once you've added the necessary configuration for both Android and iOS, you can run the app, and it will display a map centered around San Francisco, with a marker at that location.

:

Building and using Flutter packages is an essential skill for any Flutter developer. Whether you're integrating a simple UI component, performing complex data manipulation, or using third-party services like Google Maps or Firebase, Flutter's rich ecosystem of packages simplifies the process and accelerates development. By familiarizing yourself with popular packages and best practices for integrating them, you'll be able to build robust, feature-rich apps faster.

Chapter 19: Designing for Different Screen Sizes

Responsive Design Principles in Flutter

With the variety of screen sizes and resolutions available across mobile devices, designing a responsive app is crucial. Responsive design ensures that your app looks good and functions well, whether it's running on a small smartphone or a large tablet. Flutter provides several tools and techniques to help achieve a flexible, adaptive UI that responds to different screen sizes, orientations, and aspect ratios.

Here are some key principles to follow when designing for different screen sizes in Flutter:

1. **Use Flexbox Layouts (Column and Row):** The Column and Row widgets are essential for flexible layouts that adjust based on screen size. By wrapping widgets inside these containers, you can allow your UI to adapt to both smaller and larger screens dynamically.

2. **MediaQuery and LayoutBuilder:** Flutter provides two primary methods for obtaining screen dimensions and building responsive layouts:

○ **MediaQuery**: You can use MediaQuery to get information about the device's screen size, orientation, and pixel density.

Example:

dart

```
double screenWidth = MediaQuery.of(context).size.width;
double screenHeight = MediaQuery.of(context).size.height;
```

○ **LayoutBuilder**: This widget allows you to build layouts that adapt based on the parent widget's constraints. It's especially useful for creating layouts that adjust to screen size dynamically.

Example:

dart

```
LayoutBuilder(
  builder: (context, constraints) {
    if (constraints.maxWidth > 600) {
    // Tablet layout
    return Row(children: [Text('Tablet View')]);
    } else {
    // Phone layout
    return Column(children: [Text('Phone View')]);
    }
  },
```

);

3. **AspectRatio:** The AspectRatio widget helps maintain a specific aspect ratio across various screen sizes, ensuring that UI elements like images or videos maintain their proportions.

Adapting Layouts for Multiple Screen Sizes

In Flutter, you can use several techniques to ensure that your app looks great on both small and large devices:

1. **Flexible Widgets:**

   o **Expanded and Flexible**: These widgets help create layouts that expand or shrink based on available space. They are often used inside Column or Row to allow children to take up available space proportionally.

   o **Flexible**: Allows more granular control over space distribution by using the flex factor.

Example:

dart

```
Row(
 children: [
  Flexible(child: Container(color: Colors.blue)),
  Flexible(child: Container(color: Colors.green)),
```

```
    ],
    );
```

2. **Scaling with FractionallySizedBox:** This widget allows you to scale elements in relation to their parent, making it helpful for adjusting sizes proportionally.

3. **Orientation Aware Design:** Flutter provides support for detecting the screen's orientation (portrait or landscape). You can adjust layouts based on the current orientation using MediaQuery or the OrientationBuilder.

Example:

dart

```
OrientationBuilder(
  builder: (context, orientation) {
    if (orientation == Orientation.portrait) {
      return Column(children: [Text('Portrait Mode')]);
    } else {
      return Row(children: [Text('Landscape Mode')]);
    }
  },
);
```

Real-World Example: Building an App for Both Tablets and Phones

When designing an app that works well on both smartphones and tablets, it's important to consider how the layout adapts to different screen sizes. Let's look at a simple example of a product listing page that behaves differently on phones and tablets.

1. **Phone Layout**: On small screens (phones), the app displays the product list in a single column.
2. **Tablet Layout**: On larger screens (tablets), the app displays the product list in a grid or two-column layout for better use of space.

Here's an example implementation:

dart

```
import 'package:flutter/material.dart';

class ProductListingPage extends StatelessWidget {
  @override
  Widget build(BuildContext context) {
    double screenWidth = MediaQuery.of(context).size.width;

    if (screenWidth < 600) {
      // Phone layout: single-column list
      return ListView.builder(
        itemCount: 10,
        itemBuilder: (context, index) {
          return ListTile(
            title: Text('Product $index'),
            subtitle: Text('Description for product $index'),
          );
        },
```

```
  );
} else {
  // Tablet layout: two-column grid
  return GridView.builder(
    gridDelegate: SliverGridDelegateWithFixedCrossAxisCount(
      crossAxisCount: 2,  // Two columns for tablet
      childAspectRatio: 2 / 3,  // Adjust grid item aspect
    ),
    itemCount: 10,
    itemBuilder: (context, index) {
      return Card(
        child: Column(
          children: [
            Image.network('https://via.placeholder.com/150'),
            Text('Product $index'),
          ],
        ),
      );
    },
  );
 }
}
}
```

In this example, the layout dynamically changes based on the screen width:

- **Phones**: The list of products is displayed in a simple ListView.

- **Tablets**: The products are arranged in a GridView with two columns for a more spacious and responsive layout.

By using responsive design techniques, you ensure that your app adapts to various screen sizes, making it a seamless experience for users regardless of the device they're using.

Designing for different screen sizes is essential in Flutter, and the framework provides several tools to create flexible, responsive layouts. By using MediaQuery, LayoutBuilder, AspectRatio, and other responsive widgets, you can ensure that your app looks great and functions well across devices. Whether you're designing for small phones or large tablets, Flutter's adaptive layout features give you full control over how your app should behave in different screen scenarios.

Chapter 20: Animations and Transitions in Flutter

Basic Animation Techniques in Flutter

Animations are a powerful way to enhance user experience by providing smooth visual transitions between UI elements. Flutter offers a rich set of tools and widgets for creating animations, making it easy to add interactive, engaging features to your app.

In Flutter, animations can be divided into two categories: **implicit** and **explicit** animations. Each serves a different purpose and can be used depending on the complexity of the animation.

1. **Implicit Animations:**

    Implicit animations in Flutter are simpler and automatically manage the animation for you. These animations happen when a widget's properties change, and Flutter animates the change over time. You don't need to manually control the animation; just modify the property you want to animate, and Flutter handles the rest.

    Common examples of implicit animations include AnimatedContainer, AnimatedOpacity, and AnimatedPositioned.

Example - Animating a Container's size and color:

dart

```
class AnimatedExample extends StatefulWidget {
 @override
 _AnimatedExampleState createState() => _AnimatedExampleState();
}


class _AnimatedExampleState extends State<AnimatedExample> {
 double _width = 200.0;
 Color _color = Colors.blue;

 void _animate() {
  setState(() {
   _width = _width == 200.0 ? 300.0 : 200.0;
   _color = _color == Colors.blue ? Colors.red : Colors.blue;
  });
 }

 @override
 Widget build(BuildContext context) {
  return GestureDetector(
   onTap: _animate,
   child: AnimatedContainer(
    width: _width,
    height: 100,
    color: _color,
    duration: Duration(seconds: 1),
    curve: Curves.easeInOut,
    child: Center(child: Text('Tap me!')),
```

```
    ),
   );
  }
}
```

In this example, the AnimatedContainer widget animates changes to its size and color when tapped. Flutter automatically takes care of the animation, making the transition smooth.

2. Explicit Animations:

Explicit animations are more complex and offer greater control over the animation process. They allow you to define how the animation progresses over time, the duration, the curve, and even the values of the animated properties. For explicit animations, you usually work with animation controllers, tweens, and Animation objects.

Common explicit animation widgets include TweenAnimationBuilder, AnimationController, AnimatedBuilder, and Hero animations.

Example - Using an AnimationController to animate a Container's position:

dart

```
class ExplicitAnimationExample extends StatefulWidget {
  @override
```

```
  _ExplicitAnimationExampleState        createState()        =>
_ExplicitAnimationExampleState();
}


class             _ExplicitAnimationExampleState         extends
State<ExplicitAnimationExample> with TickerProviderStateMixin {
  late AnimationController _controller;
  late Animation<Offset> _animation;

  @override
  void initState() {
    super.initState();
    _controller = AnimationController(
      duration: Duration(seconds: 2),
      vsync: this,
    );

    _animation = Tween<Offset>(begin: Offset(0, 0), end: Offset(1,
0)).animate(
      CurvedAnimation(parent: _controller, curve: Curves.easeInOut),
    );
  }

  void _startAnimation() {
    _controller.forward();
  }

  @override
  Widget build(BuildContext context) {
    return Scaffold(
```

```
      appBar: AppBar(title: Text('Explicit Animation')),
      body: Center(
        child: GestureDetector(
         onTap: _startAnimation,
         child: SlideTransition(
           position: _animation,
           child: Container(
            width: 200,
            height: 100,
            color: Colors.blue,
            child: Center(child: Text('Tap to animate')),
          ),
         ),
        ),
      ),
    );
  }


  @override
  void dispose() {
   _controller.dispose();
   super.dispose();
  }
}
```

In this example, we use an AnimationController and a SlideTransition to animate the position of a Container. The animation controller manages the animation's timing, while the Tween defines the start and end positions.

Implicit vs Explicit Animations

- **Implicit Animations**: These are simple and require minimal code. Flutter automatically animates properties for you when their values change. They are typically used for simple UI transitions (e.g., resizing, fading, or changing colors).

- **Explicit Animations**: These offer more control and are used for complex animations or when you need to manipulate the animation process manually. They require more code but provide greater flexibility, such as controlling the animation duration, timing curves, and triggering multiple animations in sync.

Real-world Example: Adding Smooth Transitions to Your App

In real-world applications, smooth animations improve user experience by guiding users through app interactions, providing feedback, and making the app feel more dynamic. One common use case is animating a transition between different screens.

Example - Navigating between screens with a custom transition:

dart

```
Navigator.push(
 context,
 PageRouteBuilder(
  pageBuilder: (context, animation, secondaryAnimation) {
   return SecondScreen();
  },
```

```
transitionsBuilder: (context, animation, secondaryAnimation, child) {
  const begin = Offset(1.0, 0.0);
  const end = Offset.zero;
  const curve = Curves.easeInOut;

  var tween = Tween(begin: begin, end: end).chain(CurveTween(curve: curve));
  var offsetAnimation = animation.drive(tween);

  return SlideTransition(position: offsetAnimation, child: child);
    },
  ),
);
```

In this example, we create a custom screen transition using PageRouteBuilder. The screen slides in from the right to the left, providing a smooth, engaging transition.

Animations in Flutter are a powerful way to enhance user interactions, provide feedback, and create dynamic UIs. By mastering implicit and explicit animations, you can add a polished, professional touch to your app and improve overall usability.

Chapter 21: Custom Widgets in Flutter

Creating Reusable Custom Widgets

In Flutter, custom widgets allow you to encapsulate reusable pieces of UI into standalone, modular components. This is essential for keeping your code clean, maintainable, and scalable. Custom widgets can be composed of other widgets and can be reused throughout your app, saving development time and reducing redundancy.

To create a custom widget, you typically extend StatelessWidget or StatefulWidget and override the build() method. The key idea is to create widgets that are highly reusable and flexible, with parameters that allow customization.

Example of a Simple Custom Stateless Widget:

dart

```
class CustomCard extends StatelessWidget {
  final String title;
  final String description;
  final String imageUrl;

  CustomCard({
    required this.title,
    required this.description,
```

```dart
  required this.imageUrl,
});

@override
Widget build(BuildContext context) {
  return Card(
    elevation: 5,
    child: Column(
      crossAxisAlignment: CrossAxisAlignment.start,
      children: <Widget>[
        Image.network(imageUrl),
        Padding(
          padding: const EdgeInsets.all(8.0),
          child: Text(
            title,
            style: TextStyle(fontSize: 18, fontWeight: FontWeight.bold),
          ),
        ),
        Padding(
          padding: const EdgeInsets.all(8.0),
          child: Text(description),
        ),
      ],
    ),
  );
}
}
```

In this example:

- The CustomCard widget takes three parameters (title, description, and imageUrl), which allow it to be customized each time it's used.

- The widget encapsulates a Card that contains an image, title, and description.

This is a **StatelessWidget** because its UI is static once constructed and doesn't change unless the widget is rebuilt by the parent widget.

Understanding the Widget Tree

In Flutter, the **widget tree** is a hierarchical structure where each widget is a node, and widgets can contain other widgets as children. The widget tree is the foundation of Flutter's UI system, and the framework uses this tree to manage rendering and updates.

Every Flutter app starts with a root widget, typically MaterialApp or CupertinoApp, which provides the basic structure of the app, and from there, all other widgets are placed in the widget tree.

The widget tree is **immutable**, meaning once a widget is created, it cannot be modified directly. Instead, Flutter rebuilds the widget tree and updates the UI efficiently when the state changes.

Example of a simple widget tree structure:

dart

```
Widget build(BuildContext context) {
```

```dart
return MaterialApp(
  home: Scaffold(
    appBar: AppBar(title: Text('Custom Widget Example')),
    body: Center(
      child: CustomCard(
        title: 'Flutter Card',
        description: 'This is a simple custom card widget.',
        imageUrl: 'https://placekitten.com/200/300',
      ),
    ),
  ),
);
}
```

Here:

- MaterialApp is the root widget.
- Scaffold is a container widget that provides a structure for visual components (app bar, body, etc.).
- Center centers the CustomCard widget within the screen.

Real-world Example: A Custom Card Widget

Let's build a more complex custom widget to display a product item, such as in an e-commerce app. The widget will display an image, title, description, price, and a button to "Add to Cart."

Product Card Widget:

dart

```dart
class ProductCard extends StatelessWidget {
```

```
final String productName;
final String productDescription;
final double price;
final String imageUrl;
final VoidCallback onAddToCart;

ProductCard({
  required this.productName,
  required this.productDescription,
  required this.price,
  required this.imageUrl,
  required this.onAddToCart,
});

@override
Widget build(BuildContext context) {
  return Card(
    elevation: 8,
    shape: RoundedRectangleBorder(borderRadius: BorderRadius.circular(12)),
    child: Column(
      children: <Widget>[
        Image.network(imageUrl),
        Padding(
          padding: const EdgeInsets.all(8.0),
          child: Text(
            productName,
            style: TextStyle(fontSize: 20, fontWeight: FontWeight.bold),
          ),
        ),
        Padding(
```

```
      padding: const EdgeInsets.symmetric(horizontal: 8.0),
      child: Text(
        productDescription,
        style: TextStyle(fontSize: 14, color: Colors.grey[600]),
      ),
    ),
    Padding(
      padding: const EdgeInsets.all(8.0),
      child: Row(
        mainAxisAlignment: MainAxisAlignment.spaceBetween,
        children: <Widget>[
          Text(
            '\$$price',
            style: TextStyle(fontSize: 18, fontWeight: FontWeight.bold),
          ),
          ElevatedButton(
            onPressed: onAddToCart,
            child: Text('Add to Cart'),
          ),
        ],
      ),
    ),
  ],
  ),
);
}
}
```

Explanation of the ProductCard widget:

- **Product Info**: The widget takes parameters like product name, description, price, and image URL to display relevant product details.
- **Action**: It includes an ElevatedButton to allow the user to add the item to their cart, with a callback function (onAddToCart) that can be passed in.

Using the ProductCard widget in your app:

dart

```
ProductCard(
  productName: 'Wireless Headphones',
  productDescription: 'High-quality wireless headphones with noise cancellation.',
  price: 199.99,
  imageUrl: 'https://example.com/headphones.jpg',
  onAddToCart: () {
   print('Product added to cart!');
  },
)
```

This ProductCard widget is flexible, reusable, and customizable, making it ideal for showing multiple products in a list or grid.

Creating custom widgets in Flutter allows you to break down your app's UI into reusable, modular components. By using parameters, you can make your widgets flexible and adaptable to different scenarios. Understanding how the widget tree works in Flutter helps you organize your UI efficiently, while custom widgets help maintain clean, maintainable, and scalable code. Whether it's a simple card or a complex form, custom widgets are essential for building high-quality Flutter apps.

Chapter 22: Advanced State Management: Providers and Riverpod

---

Introduction to Advanced State Management Libraries

As your Flutter app grows in complexity, managing state efficiently becomes more challenging. Simple state management solutions like setState() may work well for small applications or isolated widgets, but for larger apps with multiple screens, complex data interactions, and shared states, more scalable solutions are needed. This is where state management libraries like **Provider** and **Riverpod** come into play.

These libraries offer powerful and flexible ways to manage state across your Flutter app, enabling better scalability, reusability, and maintainability of your code.

1. **Provider**:

   Provider is one of the most popular state management libraries in Flutter. It leverages the InheritedWidget mechanism, providing a way to propagate state down the widget tree without requiring manual passing of data between widgets. Provider is efficient, simple to use, and works well for both local and app-wide state.

Basic example of using Provider:

dart

```dart
class Counter with ChangeNotifier {
  int _count = 0;

  int get count => _count;

  void increment() {
    _count++;
    notifyListeners(); // Notifies all listening widgets to rebuild
  }
}

void main() {
  runApp(
    ChangeNotifierProvider(
      create: (_) => Counter(),
      child: MyApp(),
    ),
  );
}
```

Here, the Counter class holds the app state and notifies listeners when the value changes. ChangeNotifierProvider is used to inject the state into the widget tree.

2. **Riverpod**:

Riverpod is an advanced, more flexible alternative to Provider. It addresses some of Provider's limitations, such as making it easier to test, manage lifecycle events, and work with multiple providers simultaneously. Riverpod also doesn't depend on the widget tree, which can lead to improved performance and cleaner code.

Basic example of using Riverpod:

dart

```
final counterProvider = StateProvider<int>((ref) => 0);

void main() {
 runApp(
  ProviderScope(
   child: MyApp(),
  ),
 );
}

class MyApp extends ConsumerWidget {
 @override
 Widget build(BuildContext context, WidgetRef ref) {
  final count = ref.watch(counterProvider);
  return MaterialApp(
   home: Scaffold(
    appBar: AppBar(title: Text('Riverpod Counter')),
    body: Center(
     child: Text('$count'),
```

```
      ),
      floatingActionButton: FloatingActionButton(
        onPressed: () => ref.read(counterProvider.notifier).state++,
        child: Icon(Icons.add),
      ),
     ),
    );
   }
 }
```

Here, StateProvider is used to hold a counter value, and ConsumerWidget listens to changes in the state, automatically rebuilding when the state updates.

Real-World Example: Managing App-Wide State in a Shopping Cart App

A common use case for advanced state management is managing app-wide state, such as a shopping cart. In a shopping cart app, the state of the cart (items added, quantity, price) needs to be shared across multiple screens and easily updated as users add or remove items.

Using Provider to manage a shopping cart:

1. **Define the Cart State:**

dart

```dart
class CartItem {
  final String name;
```

```dart
  final double price;
  int quantity;

  CartItem({
    required this.name,
    required this.price,
    this.quantity = 1,
  });
}

class Cart with ChangeNotifier {
  List<CartItem> _items = [];

  List<CartItem> get items => _items;

  void addItem(CartItem item) {
    final index = _items.indexWhere((element) => element.name == item.name);
    if (index >= 0) {
      _items[index].quantity++;
    } else {
      _items.add(item);
    }
    notifyListeners();
  }

  void removeItem(CartItem item) {
    _items.remove(item);
    notifyListeners();
  }
```

```dart
double get totalPrice {
  return _items.fold(0, (sum, item) => sum + (item.price *
item.quantity));
  }
}
```

2. Set Up Provider in the Main App:

dart

```dart
void main() {
  runApp(
    ChangeNotifierProvider(
      create: (_) => Cart(),
      child: MyApp(),
    ),
  );
}
```

3. Use the Cart State in UI Components:

dart

```dart
class CartScreen extends StatelessWidget {
  @override
  Widget build(BuildContext context) {
    final cart = Provider.of<Cart>(context);
    return Scaffold(
      appBar: AppBar(title: Text('Shopping Cart')),
      body: ListView.builder(
```

```
        itemCount: cart.items.length,
        itemBuilder: (context, index) {
          final item = cart.items[index];
          return ListTile(
            title: Text(item.name),
            subtitle: Text('Quantity: ${item.quantity}'),
            trailing: Text('\$${item.price * item.quantity}'),
            onLongPress: () => cart.removeItem(item),
          );
        },
      ),
      bottomNavigationBar: Padding(
        padding: const EdgeInsets.all(8.0),
        child: Text('Total: \$${cart.totalPrice}'),
      ),
    );
  }
}
```

In this example:

- The **Cart** class holds a list of CartItem objects.
- addItem and removeItem methods modify the list and notify listeners.
- The **CartScreen** widget listens for changes to the cart state and updates the UI when items are added or removed.

By using **Provider** or **Riverpod**, you can manage the state of your shopping cart app across different screens, making it easier to maintain, scale, and test.

- **Provider** and **Riverpod** are powerful state management solutions that help manage complex app-wide states efficiently.
- **Provider** is a simple, yet effective choice for managing state that is tied to the widget tree, while **Riverpod** offers more flexibility and features, making it ideal for larger apps.
- Advanced state management libraries improve the scalability and maintainability of your Flutter apps by allowing you to separate the business logic from the UI components.

By mastering these state management tools, you can ensure that your app remains responsive, maintainable, and scalable as it grows in complexity.

Chapter 23: Testing in Flutter

Unit Testing, Widget Testing, and Integration Testing

Testing is a critical part of the software development process that helps ensure your app works as expected and remains reliable as you add new features or fix bugs. In Flutter, there are three main types of testing you'll likely work with:

1. **Unit Testing**:

   Unit tests are designed to test a single function, method, or class in isolation, without dependencies. These tests are typically fast and focus on testing the business logic or computations in your app.

   In Flutter, you use the test package to write unit tests. A simple example of unit testing a Dart function might look like this:

   dart

```
import 'package:test/test.dart';

int addNumbers(int a, int b) {
  return a + b;
}
```

```dart
void main() {
  test('addNumbers returns correct sum', () {
    expect(addNumbers(2, 3), equals(5));
  });
}
```

In this example, the addNumbers function is tested to ensure it returns the correct result.

2. **Widget Testing**:

Widget tests (also known as component tests) allow you to test individual widgets in isolation, verifying their behavior and interaction with the UI. Widget testing is useful for checking how a widget responds to user input, state changes, or interactions with other widgets.

Example of a widget test:

dart

```dart
import 'package:flutter_test/flutter_test.dart';
import 'package:flutter/material.dart';

void main() {
  testWidgets('Test button press', (WidgetTester tester) async {
    await tester.pumpWidget(MaterialApp(
      home: Scaffold(
        body: ElevatedButton(
          onPressed: () {},
          child: Text('Press Me'),
```

```
    ),
   ),
  ));
```

```
  // Verify that the button is present
  expect(find.text('Press Me'), findsOneWidget);
```

```
  // Tap the button
  await tester.tap(find.text('Press Me'));
  await tester.pump();
```

```
  // Verify any changes in the UI after the button press
  // (This could be a state change, UI update, etc.)
  });
}
```

In this example, we test a button widget to ensure it appears correctly in the UI and interacts as expected when tapped.

3. **Integration Testing**:

Integration tests focus on verifying that multiple components or features of the app work together as expected. These tests typically involve testing the entire app or larger sections of the app, such as navigating between screens, interacting with external APIs, or verifying database operations.

Integration tests in Flutter are written using the integration_test package, which allows you to interact with your entire app, simulating user input and verifying end-to-end functionality.

Example of an integration test:

dart

```
import 'package:integration_test/integration_test.dart';
import 'package:flutter_test/flutter_test.dart';
import 'package:flutter/material.dart';

void main() {
  IntegrationTestWidgetsFlutterBinding.ensureInitialized();

  testWidgets('Test navigation and button click', (tester) async {
    await tester.pumpWidget(MyApp());

    // Tap the navigation button
    await tester.tap(find.byIcon(Icons.navigate_next));
    await tester.pumpAndSettle();

    // Verify the new screen is displayed
    expect(find.text('Next Screen'), findsOneWidget);

    // Tap a button on the new screen
    await tester.tap(find.byType(ElevatedButton));
    await tester.pumpAndSettle();

    // Verify the result of the button press
    expect(find.text('Button Pressed'), findsOneWidget);
  });
```

```
}
```

This integration test simulates a complete user flow: tapping a navigation button, verifying screen changes, and checking interactions with UI elements.

Writing Tests in Dart and Flutter

Writing tests in Flutter follows a structured approach, whether you're testing Dart functions or Flutter widgets. The core testing framework is based on the test package for unit testing and the flutter_test package for widget testing.

To get started with writing tests:

1. **Unit Tests**: These are written in the test/ directory and use the test package.

2. **Widget Tests**: Also written in the test/ directory, but typically within the flutter_test framework.

3. **Integration Tests**: These are written in the integration_test/ directory and use the integration_test package.

Example Folder Structure:

bash

```
lib/
└── main.dart  # Your Flutter app code
test/
```

└── widget_test.dart # Widget testing

└── unit_test.dart   # Unit testing

integration_test/

└── app_integration_test.dart # Integration testing

To run tests:

- **Unit tests**: Run using flutter test.

- **Widget and integration tests**: Run using flutter test for widgets and flutter drive or flutter test integration_test for integration tests.

Real-World Example: Writing Tests for Your Flutter App

Let's take the example of a **Shopping Cart app**. We need to test the functionality where users can add items to the cart, remove items, and see the total price.

Unit Test for the Cart model:

dart

```
import 'package:test/test.dart';
import 'package:myapp/models/cart.dart';

void main() {
  test('Cart adds items correctly', () {
    final cart = Cart();
    cart.addItem('Apple', 1, 2.5); // Add 1 apple costing $2.5
```

```dart
    expect(cart.items.length, equals(1));
    expect(cart.totalPrice, equals(2.5));
  });

  test('Cart removes items correctly', () {
    final cart = Cart();
    cart.addItem('Apple', 1, 2.5);
    cart.removeItem('Apple');

    expect(cart.items.length, equals(0));
    expect(cart.totalPrice, equals(0.0));
  });
}
```

Widget Test for the Cart UI:

dart

```dart
import 'package:flutter_test/flutter_test.dart';
import 'package:flutter/material.dart';
import 'package:myapp/main.dart';

void main() {
  testWidgets('Add item to cart and see total', (tester) async {
    await tester.pumpWidget(MyApp());

    // Verify initial total price
    expect(find.text('Total: \$0.00'), findsOneWidget);

    // Tap the "Add to Cart" button
    await tester.tap(find.byIcon(Icons.add_shopping_cart));
    await tester.pump();
```

```
  // Verify updated total price
  expect(find.text('Total: \$2.50'), findsOneWidget);
 });
}
```

In this example:

- The **unit test** checks the cart model logic for adding and removing items.
- The **widget test** checks if the UI updates correctly when the user interacts with the app (e.g., adding an item to the cart).

By using tests, you can ensure that your app's logic and UI behave as expected, improving the reliability and stability of your Flutter application.

With these testing strategies in place, you can confidently build, test, and maintain your Flutter app, ensuring it provides the best experience for your users.

Chapter 24: Debugging and Troubleshooting Flutter Apps

Debugging Tools in Flutter and Dart

Debugging is an essential skill for developers, and Flutter provides powerful tools to help identify and resolve issues in your app. Whether you're dealing with UI glitches, logic errors, or app crashes, the right debugging techniques can save you a lot of time and frustration.

1. **Flutter DevTools**: Flutter DevTools is a suite of performance and debugging tools that help you inspect and debug your app. It includes the following key features:

   o **Widget Inspector**: Allows you to visualize the widget tree and inspect the layout.

   o **Performance Tools**: Helps you monitor CPU, memory usage, and rendering performance in real-time.

   o **Debugger**: Lets you set breakpoints, step through code, and inspect variables during execution.

2. **Dart Observatory**: Dart Observatory is a powerful tool that provides detailed performance and debugging information, especially for more complex issues related to memory usage and performance.

3. **Logging and Error Handling**:
    - **print()** **Statements**: Simple yet effective for basic debugging.
    - **debugPrint()**: Useful for larger outputs where print() might truncate the text.
    - **Error Widgets**: Use FlutterError.onError to handle uncaught Flutter framework errors.

Best Practices for Solving Common Issues

When troubleshooting a Flutter app, it's important to approach debugging systematically:

- **Check the Console**: Always start by reviewing the logs in the console for any stack traces or error messages.
- **Use Breakpoints**: Set breakpoints in your code to pause execution and inspect the state of your app.
- **Test on Multiple Devices**: Sometimes issues are device-specific, so test on different emulators and physical devices.
- **Update Dependencies**: Outdated packages or Flutter versions can sometimes cause issues—ensure everything is up-to-date using flutter pub upgrade and flutter doctor.

Real-world Example: Debugging an App that Crashes on Startup

Let's say your app crashes immediately after launch. Here's how you can debug the issue:

1. **Examine the Error Message**: Look for clues in the error log. Common causes might include null pointer exceptions, incorrect widget types, or missing dependencies.

2. **Check Dependencies**: Ensure that all required dependencies are properly installed and compatible with your Flutter version.

3. **Use Breakpoints**: Add breakpoints to the main() function and your initial widgets to pinpoint where the crash occurs.

4. **Simplify the Code**: Temporarily comment out parts of the app to narrow down the cause. Start with the most complex sections, like network calls or custom widgets, and reintroduce them gradually.

By applying these debugging tools and practices, you can quickly identify and resolve issues, ensuring a smooth experience for users.

Chapter 25: Optimizing Your Flutter App for Performance

Performance Profiling Tools

To ensure your Flutter app is running efficiently, you need to monitor its performance. Flutter provides several tools for profiling and identifying areas where your app can be optimized.

1. **Flutter DevTools:** As mentioned in Chapter 24, **DevTools** is an essential tool for profiling Flutter apps. It helps you analyze various aspects of your app's performance, including:

   o **Performance View**: This allows you to view CPU usage, memory usage, and frame rendering times. It gives you insight into how efficiently your app is running, which can highlight performance bottlenecks.

   o **Timeline**: The Timeline view allows you to examine frame rendering, identify jank (frame drops), and track asynchronous tasks.

2. **Flutter Inspector**: The **Flutter Inspector** helps analyze widget tree performance and detect layout issues. By visualizing your app's widget hierarchy, you can spot unnecessary rebuilds or inefficient layouts.

3. **DevTools Performance Page**: The Performance page gives you a comprehensive overview of CPU, GPU, and memory usage in real-time. By running your app in a profile or release mode, you can gain insights into how the app behaves under realistic conditions.

4. **Flutter's flutter run --profile Command**: Running your app in **profile mode** gives you a balance between debugging and release performance. It's ideal for measuring app performance and optimizing it before the final release.

Optimizing App Startup Time and UI Rendering

Optimizing the startup time and UI rendering of your app is crucial for delivering a smooth user experience. Here are some common strategies:

1. **Reducing App Startup Time**:

    o **Minimize work in main()**: Avoid doing heavy computations or async calls in the main() function. Instead, defer non-essential work to the first screen or screen transition.

    o **Use the Isolate API**: For computationally heavy tasks, consider using isolates, which run code on separate threads and help improve startup performance.

- **Lazy Loading of Assets**: Avoid loading all assets during startup. Load only the essential assets first and defer others to later in the app's lifecycle.

2. **Efficient Widget Rendering**: Flutter's **widget tree** rebuilds itself when the state changes. Minimizing unnecessary rebuilds can significantly improve performance.

   - **Use const Constructors**: Use const constructors wherever possible to ensure widgets don't rebuild unnecessarily.

   - **Avoid Rebuilding Large Parts of the UI**: Use the const keyword for widgets that don't change. For dynamic content, consider using ListView.builder, GridView.builder, and similar builder-based widgets, which only build visible items.

   - **Use RepaintBoundary for Optimized Painting**: If you have complex UIs or animations, you can wrap parts of the widget tree in a RepaintBoundary. This ensures only the changed parts of the UI are redrawn.

3. **Optimize the Rendering Pipeline**:

   - **Reduce Overdraw**: Overdraw occurs when a pixel is painted multiple times within a single frame. To avoid this, minimize overlapping widgets and ensure that opaque widgets don't cover transparent ones.

o **Use CachedNetworkImage**: For network images, using the CachedNetworkImage package can speed up rendering by caching images locally and avoiding unnecessary re-fetching.

o **Use Flutter's SkiaShaderMask**: For complex effects or gradients, use SkiaShaderMask to avoid costly paint operations.

Real-World Example: Making an App Faster and More Efficient

Let's say you are building a shopping app that displays a list of products. The app is lagging during the initial load and when scrolling through the product list. Here's how you could optimize it:

1. **Optimize List Performance**:

   o **Use ListView.builder**: Instead of using ListView with a static list of items, use ListView.builder to only build the items that are visible on the screen. This will reduce memory usage and improve rendering speed.

   o **Cache Images**: Use the CachedNetworkImage package to cache product images and avoid re-downloading them each time the app is opened.

2. **Lazy Loading of Data**:

- o **Pagination**: If the product list is large, implement pagination or infinite scrolling, so data is loaded in chunks. Fetch additional data only when the user scrolls to the bottom of the list, rather than loading all items at once.

3. **Minimize Initial Load Time**:
   - o **Lazy Initialization**: Defer non-essential network requests (like loading promotions or recommendations) until after the main product list is displayed.
   - o **Isolates for Heavy Tasks**: If you have heavy data processing (e.g., filtering or sorting the product list), offload this task to an isolate to avoid blocking the main thread and freezing the UI.

By applying these optimization techniques, you can improve both the performance and the user experience of your app, ensuring a smooth, fast, and responsive interface.

Key Takeaways:

- Use Flutter's **DevTools** and **Timeline** to monitor and optimize your app's performance.
- Minimize work in the **main()** function and consider lazy loading of assets and data.

- Use **ListView.builder** and **RepaintBoundary** for efficient UI rendering and to avoid unnecessary rebuilds.
- Cache assets like images to reduce network requests and improve performance.

hapter 26: Advanced Flutter Architecture Patterns

---

1. Introduction to App Architecture Patterns

- **The Importance of Architecture in Large-Scale Apps**:
  - As apps grow in complexity, maintaining a clean, scalable, and maintainable codebase becomes crucial. A strong architecture ensures your code is modular, easy to understand, and adaptable to new features or changes.

- **Common Architecture Patterns**:
  - **MVC (Model-View-Controller), MVVM (Model-View-ViewModel), BLoC (Business Logic Component), Provider & Riverpod, Redux, Clean Architecture.**

- **Why Use a Design Pattern in Flutter?**:
  - Flutter's flexibility allows developers to choose the right architecture for their needs. Patterns help separate concerns (UI, business logic, data management), making the app easier to scale and test.

2. BLoC Pattern (Business Logic Component)

- **Understanding BLoC**:
  - ○ BLoC is one of the most popular architecture patterns in Flutter for managing state. It emphasizes separating business logic from UI components, relying on streams for data communication.
  - ○ **BLoC Overview**: Core components include **Streams**, **Sinks**, and **StreamControllers**. The business logic is written inside the BLoC class, while the UI listens to streams for changes.
- **Streams and Sinks in Dart**:
  - ○ Streams are the core mechanism in BLoC for managing state and async data flow. A Stream emits data that the UI listens to, while a Sink is used to send events to the BLoC.
  - ○ Example: Building a simple counter app with BLoC that emits state changes via streams and listens for events.
- **Creating a Simple BLoC**:
  - ○ Walkthrough of implementing a simple BLoC for managing a counter state:

dart

```
class CounterBloc {
  final _counterController = StreamController<int>();
  int _counter = 0;
```

```
Stream<int>          get          counterStream          =>
_counterController.stream;

void increment() {
  _counter++;
  _counterController.sink.add(_counter);
}

void dispose() {
  _counterController.close();
}
}
```

- o **Using BLoC in the UI**: How to use StreamBuilder to connect the UI to the BLoC.

3. Provider and Riverpod: Modern State Management

- **Provider Pattern**:
  - o **What is Provider?**: Provider is a simpler and more flexible state management solution built on the concept of InheritedWidget. It allows you to manage app-wide state efficiently.
  - o Example: Using ChangeNotifierProvider to manage user authentication state across multiple screens.
- **Riverpod: The Next Evolution of Provider**:
  - o **What is Riverpod?**: Riverpod is an improved version of Provider that resolves some of the

limitations, like global state management and better support for testability.

o **Benefits of Riverpod**: Safer, more composable, and decoupled from the widget tree.

o Example: Creating a counter app using Riverpod's StateProvider.

dart

```dart
final counterProvider = StateProvider<int>((ref) => 0);

class CounterScreen extends ConsumerWidget {
  @override
  Widget build(BuildContext context, WidgetRef ref) {
    final counter = ref.watch(counterProvider);
    return Scaffold(
      appBar: AppBar(title: Text('Riverpod Counter')),
      body: Center(child: Text('$counter')),
      floatingActionButton: FloatingActionButton(
        onPressed:                    ()                    =>
ref.read(counterProvider.notifier).state++,
        child: Icon(Icons.add),
      ),
    );
  }
}
```

- **Comparing Provider and Riverpod**:

      o   Advantages of Riverpod over Provider in terms of scalability and testability.

      o   Use cases for choosing each.

4. Clean Architecture: Scalable and Maintainable Apps

- **Introduction to Clean Architecture**:
    - o **Clean Architecture** is a layered architecture that focuses on separation of concerns. It divides the app into **presentation**, **domain**, and **data** layers.
- **Core Principles**:
    - o **Independence of UI**: The UI layer depends on domain logic but not vice versa.
    - o **Testable Components**: Each layer is testable in isolation, which promotes unit testing.
- **How to Structure a Clean Architecture Flutter App**:
    - o **Entities**: Business models and core data.
    - o **Use Cases/Interactors**: Business logic and application rules.
    - o **Repositories**: Interfaces that define data sources.
    - o **Data Layer**: Contains implementations for interacting with APIs, local storage, etc.
- **Example**: A to-do app structured using Clean Architecture with separate layers for data handling, use cases, and UI. This keeps the app scalable and maintainable, even as more features are added.

5. Best Practices for Advanced Flutter Architecture

- **Decoupling UI from Business Logic**:
  - o Avoiding tight coupling between UI and logic for better scalability.
  - o Best practices for maintaining clean code (SOLID principles).

- **Choosing the Right Architecture**:
  - o When to use BLoC, Provider, Riverpod, or Clean Architecture depending on your app's needs.
  - o Considerations for small vs. large apps, and the complexity of business logic.

- **Testing and Debugging Advanced Architectures**:
  - o How to test BLoC, Riverpod, and Clean Architecture in a modular way.
  - o Debugging tips for handling app-wide state changes and asynchronous operations.

6. Real-World Example: Building a Scalable To-Do App

- **Combining Architecture Patterns**:
  - o Building a to-do app using a combination of **BLoC** for business logic, **Provider** or **Riverpod** for state management, and **Clean Architecture** for code separation.
- **Features of the App**:

o   Add, delete, and update tasks.

o   Persist tasks in local storage (e.g., SQLite).

o   Manage complex state transitions and UI updates using the chosen architecture.

o   Use **Riverpod** for app-wide state management and **BLoC** for managing task-specific logic.

This chapter will provide readers with a deeper understanding of how to build scalable and maintainable Flutter apps, offering hands-on examples of advanced architecture patterns that can be used in real-world projects. The concepts introduced here, such as **BLoC**, **Riverpod**, and **Clean Architecture**, will be essential for developers looking to build complex, professional apps with Flutter.

Chapter 27: Advanced Flutter Performance Optimization

1. Introduction to Flutter Performance Optimization

- **The Need for Performance Optimization**:
    - ○ Mobile apps must be optimized to run smoothly, especially on a wide range of devices, from entry-level smartphones to the latest flagship models. Slow apps can lead to poor user experiences and high app abandonment rates.

- **Key Areas to Optimize**:
    - ○ **Startup Time**: Ensuring the app launches quickly.
    - ○ **Rendering Performance**: Smooth UI rendering to avoid jank (frame drops).
    - ○ **Memory Usage**: Minimizing memory leaks and optimizing the app's memory footprint.

- **Flutter's Performance Tools**:
    - ○ **Flutter DevTools, Dart Observatory, Performance Profiler, Widget Inspector**.

2. Performance Profiling Tools

- **DevTools Overview**:

- o **Flutter Performance View**: Monitoring CPU usage, frame rates, and rendering performance in real-time.

- o **Timeline View**: Identifying jank, slow frames, and asynchronous task delays.

- o **Flutter Inspector**: Debugging layout issues, inspecting the widget tree, and ensuring smooth UI updates.

- **Using Dart Observatory**:

- o **Memory Usage**: Checking for memory leaks and optimizing app memory usage.

- o **CPU Profiling**: Understanding where your app is consuming the most CPU resources.

- o **Debugging Asynchronous Operations**: Profiling async tasks to prevent UI lag caused by slow background processes.

3. Optimizing App Startup Time

- **Reducing Initial Load Time**:

- o **Lazy Loading**: Loading only the essential components at startup and deferring other resources.

- o **Deferred Imports**: Using deferred loading to import only when required.

- **Flutter's Native Code Compilation**:

- o **Reducing Cold Startup Latency**: Ensuring the app doesn't take too long to initialize.

- o **Improving Hot Restart Performance**: Leveraging Flutter's hot-reload for faster iteration during development.

- **Minimizing the Main Thread Workload**:

  - o **Isolate Usage**: Offloading work to background isolates for more responsive UI.

4. Optimizing UI Rendering

- **Widget Tree Optimization**:

  - o **Avoiding Unnecessary Rebuilds**: Using const constructors and RepaintBoundary to optimize widget tree rebuilds.

  - o **Effective State Management**: Using efficient state management approaches like BLoC, Provider, or Riverpod to minimize unnecessary state updates.

- **Efficient Layouts**:

  - o **Avoiding Nested Widgets**: Reducing complexity in the widget tree to improve rendering time.

  - o **Using ListView.builder and GridView.builder**: Dynamically creating only the visible items in a list or grid to improve memory and rendering performance.

- **Custom Painting and Complex Animations**:

- o **CustomPainter**: Using CustomPainter for advanced drawing tasks without causing excessive rendering overhead.

- o **Optimizing Animation Performance**: Using AnimatedBuilder, reducing the number of animated properties, and minimizing unnecessary redraws.

5. Optimizing Memory Usage

- **Detecting and Fixing Memory Leaks**:
  - o **Memory Profiling**: Using Flutter DevTools to monitor memory usage and identify leaks.
  - o **Weak References and Garbage Collection**: Understanding how Dart's garbage collection works and ensuring objects are disposed of properly.

- **Reducing Memory Footprint**:
  - o **Asset Optimization**: Compressing images and reducing the size of assets like fonts and icons to save memory.
  - o **Efficient Data Caching**: Implementing caching strategies to minimize network calls and reduce memory overhead.

6. Real-World Example: Making an E-commerce App Faster

- **Scenario Overview**:

- o In this example, we'll look at an e-commerce app that has performance issues due to slow startup times, janky animations, and high memory usage.

- **Optimizing Startup Time**:
  - o Using deferred loading for product images and data, and lazy loading for the main dashboard.

- **Improving UI Rendering**:
  - o Using ListView.builder for dynamically loading product items, reducing widget rebuilds, and optimizing animations for smooth transitions when adding items to the cart.

- **Optimizing Memory Usage**:
  - o Reducing the size of product images, caching network requests, and removing unnecessary large assets.

7. Best Practices for Maintaining Performance in Large Apps

- **Adopting Continuous Performance Monitoring**:
  - o Using performance profiling tools during development and after release to identify regressions and new issues.

- **Code Reviews and Performance Audits**:
  - o Establishing code review practices that focus on performance, especially when adding new features or modifying the UI.

- **Automated Performance Testing**:
  - Integrating performance tests into the CI/CD pipeline to catch performance issues before they reach production.

8.

- **Balancing Performance with Features**:
  - As an app grows, achieving a balance between adding new features and maintaining performance is key. Performance optimization should be an ongoing process, not a one-time effort.
- **The Role of Profiling and Tools**:
  - Emphasizing the importance of using tools like Flutter DevTools, Dart Observatory, and various profiling techniques to ensure your app delivers the best possible user experience.

- Performance optimization is critical for delivering fast, smooth, and responsive apps.
- Flutter provides powerful profiling tools to monitor and improve app performance, including startup time, UI rendering, and memory usage.
- By applying best practices for widget tree optimization, layout design, and memory management, you can

significantly enhance app performance, ensuring that your Flutter app runs efficiently on all devices.

This chapter serves as a deep dive into optimizing Flutter app performance, ensuring that as your app scales, it continues to deliver a fast, responsive, and seamless user experience.

Chapter 28: Implementing Secure and Scalable Flutter Apps

---

1. Introduction to Security and Scalability in Flutter Apps

- **Why Security and Scalability Matter**:
    - Security ensures that user data is protected and prevents vulnerabilities like data breaches or unauthorized access.
    - Scalability ensures that the app can handle increased traffic, data, and functionality as it grows, without compromising performance or stability.
- **Common Security Risks in Mobile Apps**:
    - Data breaches, insecure data storage, network attacks, and improper authentication mechanisms.
- **Common Challenges in Scalability**:
    - Handling large amounts of data, optimizing API calls, managing user load, and ensuring smooth performance during traffic spikes.

2. Secure Data Handling in Flutter

- **Secure Storage**:

- o Using packages like flutter_secure_storage to store sensitive data securely on the device.
- o Best practices for storing passwords, API tokens, and other sensitive information.

- **Data Encryption**:
  - o Implementing encryption techniques to protect data both at rest and in transit.
  - o Introduction to libraries like encrypt for implementing AES encryption in Flutter.

- **Network Security**:
  - o Implementing SSL pinning to secure network requests.
  - o Using HTTPS and securing API communication.
  - o Avoiding hardcoded credentials and using environment variables or secure vaults.

3. Implementing Scalable State Management

- **State Management for Scalability**:
  - o Overview of **Provider**, **Riverpod**, and **BLoC** for managing state across large, complex Flutter apps.
  - o Choosing the right state management approach depending on the app's size, features, and the team's needs.

- o Best practices for efficient state management to avoid unnecessary rebuilds and reduce app memory usage.
- **Handling Large Data Sets Efficiently**:
  - o Techniques for working with large data in Flutter (pagination, lazy loading, and efficient list rendering).
  - o Using ListView.builder and GridView.builder for optimal performance when displaying long lists.
  - o Handling data storage and retrieval efficiently with **SQLite** or **Firebase**.

4. Optimizing Backend Integration for Scalability

- **Using Firebase for Scalability**:
  - o Leveraging Firebase's real-time database, Firestore, and Firebase Authentication for handling large user bases.
  - o Benefits of using Firebase for managing real-time data syncing and offline capabilities.
- **GraphQL for Scalable Data Queries**:
  - o Overview of **GraphQL** and how it allows efficient data querying, minimizing the amount of data transferred over the network.
  - o Integrating GraphQL with Flutter using the graphql_flutter package.

- **API Rate Limiting and Caching**:
  - o Implementing API rate limiting to ensure that your app doesn't overload your backend.
  - o Using local caching (e.g., with Hive or SQLite) to minimize unnecessary network requests and improve performance.

5. Ensuring App Security with Authentication and Authorization

- **Implementing Secure Authentication**:
  - o Using Firebase Authentication, OAuth 2.0, or custom JWT-based authentication systems to handle user login and sign-up securely.
  - o Implementing multi-factor authentication (MFA) for added security.
- **Role-based Access Control**:
  - o Managing different levels of access within the app to ensure users can only access resources they're authorized to.
  - o Implementing role-based access control (RBAC) in Flutter with Firebase or custom backends.

6. Scaling the Flutter App UI for Multiple Devices

- **Responsive Design Principles**:

- o Creating layouts that adjust to different screen sizes (phones, tablets, and web) using MediaQuery, LayoutBuilder, and the Flexible and Expanded widgets.
- o Best practices for designing flexible UIs using Flutter's rich set of layout widgets.

- **Adaptive Layouts for Different Screen Resolutions**:
  - o Ensuring that your app provides a consistent user experience across various devices and screen densities.
  - o Handling high-density screens (e.g., Retina displays) and low-density screens by providing appropriate assets and UI adjustments.

7. Monitoring and Logging for Secure and Scalable Apps

- **App Monitoring Tools**:
  - o Integrating monitoring tools like **Firebase Crashlytics**, **Sentry**, and **New Relic** to track app performance, crash reports, and user behavior.
  - o Setting up custom logging for tracking app errors and security breaches.
- **Real-time Analytics for Scaling**:
  - o Leveraging tools like **Firebase Analytics** and **Google Analytics** to monitor user behavior and identify scaling needs.

o Using the insights from analytics to improve app performance and security measures.

8. : Best Practices for Building Secure and Scalable Flutter Apps

- **Continuous Integration and Continuous Deployment (CI/CD)**:
  - o Setting up CI/CD pipelines for automated testing, building, and deploying Flutter apps securely.
  - o Best practices for maintaining a smooth deployment pipeline with services like GitHub Actions or GitLab CI.
- **Security Best Practices**:
  - o Always encrypt sensitive data.
  - o Secure API endpoints using HTTPS, OAuth, or JWT.
  - o Implement proper error handling to avoid exposing sensitive information.
- **Scalability Best Practices**:
  - o Design your app to handle increased load by optimizing backend communication and using cloud services like Firebase or AWS.
  - o Monitor app performance and make incremental improvements to maintain a smooth user experience.

This chapter would serve as a comprehensive guide for implementing both **security** and **scalability** in a production-ready Flutter app. It would give readers the knowledge they need to ensure their apps can grow seamlessly, support a large user base, and keep sensitive data secure.

Chapter 29: Deploying and Maintaining Flutter Apps

---

1. Introduction to App Deployment and Maintenance

- **Why Deployment and Maintenance Matter**:
    - Deployment is the process of distributing your app to users, while maintenance ensures that it continues to work smoothly after release. Effective deployment and maintenance strategies can ensure long-term success for your app.
- **Common Challenges in Deployment and Maintenance**:
    - App compatibility across different devices and OS versions, handling updates, managing user feedback, and fixing bugs in production.

2. Preparing Your Flutter App for Release

- **Preparing for iOS Deployment**:
    - **Provisioning Profiles and Certificates**: Setting up necessary credentials in Xcode for signing the app.
    - **App Store Connect**: How to configure and upload your app to the App Store, including filling out metadata and screenshots.

- o **App Review Guidelines**: Understanding Apple's app review process and how to avoid common rejection reasons.
- **Preparing for Android Deployment**:
  - o **Creating a Release Build**: Generating a signed APK or AAB file for release using Flutter's build commands.
  - o **Google Play Console**: Setting up your app on Google Play, configuring pricing, distribution, and beta testing.
  - o **Optimizing for Google Play Store**: Tips for creating effective store listings, using app bundles, and optimizing app size for better download performance.

3. Continuous Integration and Continuous Deployment (CI/CD)

- **Setting Up CI/CD Pipelines for Flutter**:
  - o Integrating Flutter with popular CI/CD platforms like **GitHub Actions**, **Bitrise**, or **Codemagic** to automate builds, tests, and deployments.
- **Automating App Releases**:
  - o How CI/CD pipelines can automatically trigger new builds when code is pushed to repositories, run tests, and deploy your app to app stores or internal testers.
- **Testing and Deployment Workflow**:

    ○ Automated testing (unit, widget, integration tests) as part of the CI pipeline to ensure that new features or bug fixes don't break the app.

4. Post-Deployment Maintenance

- **Monitoring App Performance**:
  - ○ Using tools like **Firebase Crashlytics**, **Sentry**, and **Flutter DevTools** to monitor app performance, track errors, and analyze crash reports.
  - ○ **Tracking Key Metrics**: Monitor user behavior, app crashes, and other key performance indicators (KPIs) to identify and address issues.

- **User Feedback and Bug Fixing**:
  - ○ How to collect and prioritize user feedback from app reviews, social media, and analytics to fix bugs and enhance the app.
  - ○ **Over-the-Air (OTA) Updates**: Techniques for pushing small updates, bug fixes, or content changes without requiring users to download a new app version (using services like **CodePush** or **Flutter's hot reload** feature).

- **App Updates**:
  - ○ Planning and rolling out app updates, including introducing new features, fixing bugs, and ensuring backward compatibility for existing users.

5. Best Practices for Ongoing App Maintenance

- **App Versioning**:
  - Proper versioning practices for releasing updates (e.g., following **semantic versioning**).
  - How to handle major vs. minor updates and ensure smooth transitions for users.
- **Backwards Compatibility**:
  - Managing changes in APIs and features while ensuring the app remains compatible with older OS versions and devices.
- **Managing App Store Reviews**:
  - Monitoring and responding to user reviews in both **Google Play Store** and **Apple App Store**.
  - Using reviews to identify pain points and prioritize fixes.

6. Final Thoughts and Future of Flutter App Deployment

- **Future Trends in Mobile App Deployment**:
  - The rise of **App Clips** and **Progressive Web Apps (PWAs)** in the mobile ecosystem.
  - The evolving landscape of **cross-platform development** and Flutter's role in it.
- **Staying Up-to-Date**:

o   Keeping your Flutter knowledge current by regularly checking for updates in Flutter's official documentation and developer tools.

o   Participating in the Flutter community (e.g., **Flutter Devs** on GitHub, StackOverflow, and Reddit).

: In this chapter, we've explored how to effectively deploy your Flutter app to both **iOS** and **Android**, optimize the release process, automate deployments with **CI/CD** tools, and handle ongoing maintenance tasks like monitoring performance, addressing user feedback, and managing app updates. Mastering these deployment and maintenance strategies ensures that your Flutter app is reliable, efficient, and continues to evolve after its initial release.